the complete series

BAKING

hinkler

Published by Hinkler Books Pty Ltd
45–55 Fairchild Street
Heatherton Victoria 3202 Australia
www.hinkler.com.au

Text and images © Anthony Carroll 2011
Design © Hinkler Books Pty Ltd 2012

Recipes on page 11, 15, 16, 19, 20, 31 and 32 were provided by
Tarmara Milstein: tamara@tamaraskitchen.com

Cover design: Hinkler Design Studio
Typesetting: MPS Limited
Prepress: Graphic Print Group

ISBN: 978 1 7430 8641 4

Printed and bound in China

CONTENTS

INTRODUCTION

Baking has been with us for thousands of years, originating with the ancient Babylonians. Their techniques for baking bread were adopted by the ancient Egyptians and ancient Greeks and, by Roman times, banqueting tables groaned under tasty pastries, tortes and doughnut-like breads.

Unlike other cooking methods that rely upon radiant heat, baking utilises the dry heat of convection which can also be achieved using hot ashes or stones. Many of the ancient bakers began by smothering dough in such heated materials or shaping paste onto a hot rock. But the baker's craft has really come into its own since developing into an oven-based cuisine.

With advances in modern ovenware, more and more baked treats that had formerly been the preserve of master bakers and caterers can be produced in the home. Nowadays, many modern homes include state-of-the-art catering ovens – but even the advent of the basic oven has allowed home cooks to add increasingly sophisticated baked goods to their repertoires.

For baby-boomers, the soufflé was a floaty, French dessert only ever attempted by the brave or foolhardy, so uncertain was the likelihood of a successful outcome. Now, modern cooks can bake with greater confidence, although it is advisable to get to know your own oven as heat can vary from one unit to another. The many available settings, such as fan-forced, can also affect baking time and result.

Instinctively, we feel that there is something comforting and earthy about anything that is home-baked. Perhaps it is because few cooked foods have the ability to transport us back to our childhoods like the smell of freshly baked goods. For many of us, baked treats are comfort foods, harking back to treats that Grandma used to make. Cupcakes, hot cross buns, pies – each has the power to elicit fond memories of the past and lift our spirits in the present. They are a favourite among kids and adults alike. With this book, you have the power to create new baked favourites in your own house.

Breads

Almost every culture bakes some sort of bread. French boulangers are prolific bakers. They brought their highly enriched eggy brioche to the culinary table. And who could be without that much-loved buttery pastry, the croissant, not to mention the ubiquitous crusty French baguette. Similarly, an Indian meal is virtually incomplete without a

chapati to scoop it up with. Turkey has brought us the pide bread, that fabulously versatile flatbread that is the mainstay of any dipping platter. Other less traditional breads include soda bread, herbed beer bread and Australian damper that is enjoyed with golden (corn) syrup.

Pies and tarts

Savoury pies can make a satisfying and delicious meal or snack – from the substantial beef and mushroom pie to individual meat pies to delectable meat-filled Cornish pasties. The versatility of a finely rolled, crumbly pastry also perfectly accommodates a sweet filling, such as fruit pies and spicy pumpkin pie. Of course, open-faced pies – tarts – are the perfect vehicle for a sweet filling: rhubarb and apple tart, raspberry and hazelnut tarts, and fresh fruit tartlets are all here for you to enjoy.

Desserts, cakes and cheesecakes

You will dazzle your dinner party guests with desserts like pavlova, named because of its light texture for the Russian ballerina Ánna Pávlova. Or whip up our effortless orange liqueur soufflé or bake the tangy citrus delicious pudding – either would be a sophisticated finale to any dinner. For something more home-style, try the humble apple and rhubarb crumble – perfect with cream or ice-cream.

Cakes form a central part of virtually every event, but you can bake a cake with no excuse at all except for wanting to satisfy a sweet tooth. The classic spiced apple cake and orange poppy seed cake are perennial favourites, while raspberry chocolate truffle cakes will bring a wow factor to your next afternoon tea. Why not put on a proper high tea with the spongey goodness of the Victoria sandwich cake, replete with jam and cream, as its centrepiece.

Cheesecakes need not only be plain cream cheese and a biscuit crust: try the zesty combinations of citrus in our orange and lime cheesecake or enjoy the rich decadence of toffee cheesecake. The chocolate caramel cheesecake is likely to become a family dessert mainstay and the mini passionfruit cheesecakes will give cupcakes a run for their money with the kids. For more mature tastes, try the plum and bitter orange cheesecake or the adults-only fruit and bourbon cheesecake.

Cookies, slices and squares

Shop-bought cookies cannot compare to cookies baked at home. Fresh-baked cookies are both crisp and moist, a dimension that cookies from a packet can seldom achieve. Bake a batch and keep them in an airtight container for snack breaks ... that's if they last that long once the family smells these freshly baked treats! Try the delectable combination of peanut butter and honey cookies, keep some almond biscotti on hand to have with after-dinner coffees, and be sure to have some pecan crispies for the kids' afternoon tea.

It is so easy to whip up slices or squares. You can keep them in a container in the fridge for when unexpected guests drop by. They will impress visitors in a way that a packet of cookies never can. The kids will love the lamingtons and caramel squares while the older folks won't be able to stop at one chocolate rum slice or the almond-flavoured baklava.

Shortbread, scones and buns

Shortbread comes in a much wider variety of flavours and shapes than you may expect. From chocolate shortbread to simple shortbread cookies, they are the perfect Christmas gift that is gratefully received the whole year round.

Steep some tea, whip some cream and scoop some of your favourite jam into a dish. All that remains is to make a batch of our traditional scone recipe and you have put together a Devonshire tea to rival any tea room. Some scone aficionados never go past plain scones with jam and cream, however, there are a range of fabulous scone varieties you can experiment with in this book. Scones with currants, apple, ginger, dates and even cheese. This is not to mention the scone's cousin, the hot cross bun, which is surprisingly easy to bake any time of year.

Muffins and cupcakes

Muffins are generally larger than cupcakes and can even substitute for them. They can be as sweet and satisfying as raspberry muffins or as savoury as cheese and bacon muffins. They can also stand in for cereal as a breakfast on the run. Muffins lend themselves to the use of different grains such as wholemeal (whole wheat) flour and oat bran, as well as dried fruits, which encourage intestinal health.

Holding a kids' party? There is no better way to entertain a group of children than by baking a batch of cupcakes and getting the kids to ice them themselves. Set up a table of different frostings and decorations and let them loose! It is both an involving activity and one that guarantees a yummy finale. It is also something you can do at home – better yet, involve your kids in the baking process. It will become a lifelong memory for all of you.

The reason for the continued popularity of home-baking is twofold: the creative satisfaction of making baked goods yourself is difficult to beat; it is also a

form of culinary generosity. Cooking food for others is an act of love and, with baking in particular, a little love is baked into every bite! Baking is sharing that love. It is no coincidence that the nurturing act of growing a baby is known colloquially as having 'a bun in the oven'.

BREADS

They say that the best way to sell a house is to bake bread. A house filled with the smell of a freshly baked loaf on the day of the inspection instantly converts a house into a home. The crunchy crust and soft, pillowy interior of a buttery slice of bread fresh from the oven is something that a shop-bought loaf simply cannot match.

COUNTRY CORNBREAD

1 cup polenta (cornmeal)
1 cup plain (all-purpose) flour
2 tablespoons sugar
1 tablespoon baking powder
½ teaspoon salt
¾ cup milk
½ cup sour cream
2 eggs
100g/3½ oz butter, melted

1   Preheat oven to 180°C/360°F.

2   In a large mixing bowl, stir together all the dry ingredients. Mix the milk, sour cream, eggs and butter separately and blend well. Mix with the flour mixture until just combined.

3   Pour the batter into a well-oiled square cake tin, about 23 x 23cm/9 x 9 in. Bake for approximately 30 minutes until a skewer inserted into the bread comes out clean. Cut into squares or rectangles and serve warm.

Cornbread is a deliciously soft bread, served cut into squares and most commonly eaten with savoury dishes like chilli con carne and casseroles that have a gravy. It has been very popular in America for centuries, often eaten for breakfast with eggs and sausages. This recipe is an updated version, with sour cream included for extra richness.

Serves 8 · Preparation 15 minutes · Cooking 30 minutes

SODA BREAD

500g/1 lb plain (all-purpose) flour
1 teaspoon bicarbonate of soda (baking soda)
1 teaspoon salt
45g/1½ oz butter
2 cups buttermilk or milk

1   Preheat oven to 200°C/400°F.
2   Sift the flour, bicarbonate of soda (baking soda) and salt into a bowl. Rub in the
    butter, using your fingertips, until the mixture resembles coarse breadcrumbs.
    Make a well in the centre of the flour mixture, pour in the milk or buttermilk and,
    using a round-ended knife, mix to form a soft dough.
3   Turn dough onto a floured surface and knead lightly until smooth. Shape into
    an 18cm/7 in round and place on a buttered and floured baking tray (sheet).
    Score dough into eighths using a sharp knife. Dust lightly with flour and bake for
    35–40 minutes or until the loaf sounds hollow when tapped on the base.

Serves 8 · Preparation 15 minutes · Cooking 40 minutes

BASIL BEER BREAD

2 cups self-raising flour, sifted
60g/2 oz sugar
¾ cup fresh basil, chopped
1 teaspoon crushed black peppercorns
1 cup beer, at room temperature

1   Preheat oven to 180°C/360°F.
2   Place flour, sugar, basil, peppercorns and beer in a bowl and mix to make a
    soft dough.
3   Place dough in a buttered and lined 10 x 20cm/4 x 8 in loaf tin and bake for
    50 minutes or until bread is cooked when tested with a skewer.
4   Stand bread in the tin for 5 minutes before turning onto a wire rack to cool.
    Serve warm or cold.

This bread is delicious spread with olive or sun-dried tomato paste. Any beer
may be used; you can experiment with light and dark ales and even stout to
achieve different results.

Makes one loaf · Preparation 15 minutes · Cooking 50 minutes

CROISSANTS

7–8 cups unbleached bread flour
1 level tablespoon malt extract
4 tablespoons sugar
2 teaspoons salt
2 tablespoons yeast
2 tablespoons evaporated milk
500g/1 lb unsalted butter, chilled

1 Place all ingredients except butter and 2 tablespoons of warm water in a mixing
   bowl and combine with a wooden spoon. When ingredients begin to stick together,
   turn out mass of dough and knead mixture gently on a well-floured surface until
   all ingredients are incorporated and dough is smooth and elastic (about 10 minutes).
   Shape into a square, flour well and place on a flat oven tray (sheet), covered loosely
   with plastic wrap. Place in refrigerator for a minimum of 2 hours, or overnight.

2 When chilled, remove dough from refrigerator and roll out to a rectangular shape
   approximately 30 x 60cm/12 x 24 in. Using a vegetable peeler or cheese slicer, cut
   slices of chilled butter and lay them on bottom two thirds of dough.

3 Carefully seal seam, turn dough so seam is at the side and gently but firmly roll
   out dough to a large rectangle. Fold dough as before, bringing top third down and
   the bottom third up, then flour well and place on tray and chill for at least 2 hours.
   Repeat the above rolling, buttering, folding and rolling process again, using remaining
   butter. Again, chill for a minimum of 2 hours.

4 When ready to shape croissants, flour bench well. Firmly but gently roll out dough
   to a thickness of about 3mm/⅛ in and about 60 x 40cm/24 x 16 in. With a sharp
   knife, cut dough in half so that you have two pieces each 60 x 20cm/24 x 8 in.

5 Mark out triangles with base of about 8cm/3 in and height of 20cm/8 in so that
   full width of dough is used and each triangle joins the one before, with no wastage.
   Cut out these triangles. Place a small cut in middle of base of each triangle then roll
   triangles up gently but firmly, from base towards point of triangle. Continue rolling
   croissants up to form croissant shape and place them on an oiled oven tray, making
   sure that point lies under the croissant.

6 Gently curve corners to resemble a croissant. Allow to rise until doubled in size and
   carefully glaze with milk. Allow to rest 30 minutes. Preheat oven to 240°C/460°F, then
   bake for about 10 minutes, watching for signs of burning. When baked, cool on wire rack.

Serves 6 · Preparation 8 hours · Cooking 30 minutes

FRENCH OLIVE LADDER BREAD

1 tablespoon yeast
4 cups bread flour
2 cups wholemeal (whole wheat) flour
¼ cup buckwheat flour
2 tablespoons olive oil
2 teaspoons sea salt
1–2 cups black (ripe) olives, chopped

1   Preheat oven to 200°C/400°F.

2   Combine yeast, 3 cups warm water and 2 cups bread flour and mix well with a wooden spoon for 3 minutes, until mixture resembles a thick batter. Cover with plastic wrap and allow to rest for 2–3 hours at room temperature.

3   Add all remaining ingredients and mix to form a soft dough. Turn out onto a floured bench and knead well for about 10 minutes, adding a little extra flour if dough is too sticky. Return dough to an oiled bowl and allow to rise once more for 1 hour.

4   Remove dough from bowl and divide into four even pieces. Working with one piece at a time, flatten dough to a thickness of 12mm/½ in and approximately 30 x 10cm/12 x 4 in. With a sharp knife, make deep cuts in dough 12mm/½ in inside each edge and extending from one side of dough to other. When you have made four cuts, gently pull top and bottom of dough to stretch cuts, making cuts look like rungs on a ladder. Complete other pieces of dough in same manner. Transfer breads to oiled baking trays (sheets) and allow to rise for 30 minutes at room temperature. Brush with olive oil and scatter a little sea salt over surface.

5   Bake for 20–25 minutes, until loaves are crisp and golden.

Serves 6 • Preparation 4 hours • Cooking 25 minutes

FRENCH BAGUETTES

1 tablespoon dried yeast
1 tablespoon sugar
1 tablespoon salt
5–6 cups unbleached bread flour
1 egg white, beaten

1   Preheat oven to 220°C/430°F.

2   Mix yeast, sugar, salt and 4 cups of flour with 2 cups warm water. Add remaining
    flour, half a cup at a time, until dough is very soft but still manageable enough to
    knead. Turn dough out onto a floured surface and incorporate only as much flour
    as is needed to prevent sticking, then knead very well until dough is soft and satiny.
    Place in oiled bowl and allow to rise until doubled in size (about 2 hours). If you
    have time, this dough would benefit from a longer rise.

3   Turn dough out and cut into three or four equal portions (depending on required
    size of baguettes). Roll dough out to an oval shape and roll up tightly, Swiss-roll
    fashion. Roll shaped dough back and forth to lengthen baguette.

4   Brush surface with beaten egg white or water then sprinkle with flour. With a very
    sharp knife, slash tops of baguettes diagonally at 10cm/4 in intervals and allow
    dough to rise at room temperature until doubled in size (about 30 minutes). Bake
    for 20–30 minutes until crisp and pale golden.

Serves 4 · Preparation 3 hours · Cooking 30 minutes

DAMPER

1 cup wholemeal (whole wheat) self-raising flour
1 cup white self-raising flour
1¼ cups skim milk
1 teaspoon dry mustard
1 tablespoon sesame seeds

1 Prehat oven to 200°C/400°F.

2 Sift flour into a bowl, return husks from sifter to bowl. Stir in enough skim milk to give a sticky dough. Knead on lightly floured surface until smooth, shape into a round.

3 Place dough onto lightly buttered oven tray (sheet), press out with fingers to about 25mm/1 in thick. Using a sharp knife, mark into wedges, cut wedges into dough about 12mm/½ in deep.

4 Sprinkle dough with combined mustard and sesame seeds. Bake for 30 minutes or until golden brown and damper sounds hollow when tapped with fingers.

Makes one loaf · Preparation 20 minutes · Cooking 30 minutes

PIDE

3⅓ cups plain (all-purpose) flour
7g/¼ oz dry yeast
pinch of salt
1 teaspoon sugar
2 tablespoons olive oil
1 egg, lightly beaten
⅓ cup sesame seeds

1 Preheat oven to 220°C/430°F.

2 Combine flour, yeast, salt and sugar in a bowl. Make a well in the centre. Stir in 1½ cups warm water and the oil. Mix to make a soft dough. Knead on a lightly floured surface for 10 minutes, adding more flour as needed, until soft, elastic and smooth. Place in a lightly oiled bowl. Turn to coat with oil. Cover. Stand in a warm place for 1 hour or until doubled in size.

3 Punch down. Divide into two equal portions. Roll each portion into a ball. Cover with tea towel. Stand in a warm place for 20–30 minutes.

4 Flatten each ball to make a 25cm/10 in circle. Pull into an oval shape. Place on a lightly buttered baking tray (sheet). Make indentations over surface with fingertips, leaving a 25mm/1 in border. Brush generously with egg. Sprinkle with sesame seeds.

5 Bake for 15 minutes or until golden. Wrap in a tea towel. Cool.

Makes 18 pieces • Preparation 2 hours • Cooking 15 minutes

HERBED BEER BREAD

2 cups plain (all-purpose) flour
1 teaspoon bicarbonate of soda (baking soda)
45g/1½ oz Parmesan cheese, grated
2 tablespoons pitted black (ripe) olives, chopped
2 tablespoons olive oil
¾ cup beer
¾ cup chopped mixed fresh herbs, for example, parsley, basil,
coriander (cilantro) and oregano

1   Preheat oven to 180°C/360°F.

2   Combine flour, bicarbonate of soda (baking soda), Parmesan cheese and olives
    in a bowl. Make a well in the centre. Mix in oil and enough beer to make a
    moist dough.

3   Spoon one third of the dough into a buttered 8 x 20cm/3 x 8 in loaf tin. Sprinkle
    with one half of the herbs. Top with one third of the remaining dough. Sprinkle
    with remaining herbs. Top with remaining dough. Brush with a little milk.

4   Bake for 1 hour or until base sounds hollow when tapped.

Makes 16 slices • Preparation 20 minutes • Cooking 1 hour

CHAPATIS

250g/9 oz wholemeal (whole wheat) flour
1 teaspoon salt

1   Sift flour and salt into a bowl. Make a well in the centre and add 1 cup of water, a little at a time, using your fingers to incorporate the surrounding flour to make a smooth, pliable dough.

2   Knead dough on a lightly floured surface for 5–10 minutes, then place in a bowl, cover with a cloth and leave to rest for 30–60 minutes.

3   Knead dough for 2–3 minutes. Divide into 6 balls of equal size, then flatten each ball into a circle, about 12cm/5 in in diameter.

4   Heat an unbuttered frying pan (skillet) until hot. Place one chapati at a time on hot surface. As soon as bubbles appear on surface of chapati, turn the chapati over. Press down on chapati with a thick cloth so that it cooks evenly.

5   To finish chapati, lift it with a fish slice and hold it carefully over an open gas flame without turning until it puffs up slightly. Alternatively, place the chapati under a hot grill (broiler).

6   Repeat with remaining dough circles. Keep cooked chapatis hot in a covered napkin-lined basket.

Makes 15 · Preparation 1 hour · Cooking 30 minutes

FRENCH SOURDOUGH WITH CARAMELISED ONIONS

1 cup wholemeal (whole wheat) flour
1 cup natural yoghurt
1 teaspoon sugar
1 teaspoon yeast
45g/1½ oz butter
4 large onions, sliced
1 tablespoon dried yeast
1 teaspoon sugar
1½ teaspoons salt
1 teaspoon bicarbonate of soda (baking soda)
2–3 cups wholemeal (whole wheat) flour, extra

1   In a large mixing bowl, combine wholemeal (whole wheat) flour, yoghurt, sugar, yeast and ¼ cup warm water. Mix well, then set aside and allow to ferment at room temperature for 24 hours.

2   The next day, melt butter in large frying pan (skillet) and add sliced onions. Stir to coat with butter and cook over medium heat until onions are translucent. Cover saucepan with lid and continue to cook on low heat for about 40 minutes or until onions are golden brown. Set aside to cool.

3   Mix yeast, ¼ cup warm water and sugar together and allow to sit for 5 minutes. Mix this mixture into prepared starter dough along with salt, half the caramelised onions and the bicarbonate of soda (baking soda). Slowly add more flour until dough forms a shaggy mass.

4   When dough is quite smooth and manageable, allow it to rise for 30 minutes at room temperature. Remove dough from bowl and divide in half. Shape each piece of dough into a flat oval loaf about 12mm/½ in thick, using your fingertips to add texture to dough. Scatter remaining onions over surface of dough then drizzle dough with some olive oil and allow to rest again for 30 minutes. Preheat oven to 200°C/400°F. Spray dough with water and bake for 25–30 minutes, or until crusty and golden.

Serves 6 · Preparation 1 hour, plus standing time · Cooking 30 minutes

FOUGASSE PROVENÇALE

2 cups bread flour
1 large tablespoon yeast
1½ kg/3 lb plain (all-purpose) flour
1½ tablespoons salt
1 tablespoon yeast
8 cloves garlic, freshly minced
⅓ cup olive oil

1   To make starter, mix flour, yeast and water together until mixture resembles a
    semi-thick batter. Allow to prove, covered, in a non-reactive bowl for up to 3 days
    (8 hours minimum) to develop a lovely mature flavour.

2   To make dough, mix the starter, 1 kg of flour, salt, yeast, garlic and half the oil with
    1 cup of warm water to make a soft dough. Knead on floured surface until dough
    is silky smooth, adding remaining flour as necessary until dough is no longer sticky.
    Allow dough to rise at room temperature in an oiled bowl until doubled in size
    (about 2 hours).

3   Divide dough into 12 pieces and, using your fingertips or rolling pin, shape into
    ovals about 1cm/⅓ in thick. With a sharp knife, make diagonal cuts through dough
    and then gently stretch to open up holes. Brush with remaining oil and sprinkle
    with a little sea salt if desired.

4   Preheat oven to 100°C/210°F. Allow dough to rise for 30 minutes at room
    temperature then bake for 15–20 minutes, spraying with water twice during baking
    (if you prefer, place baking pan of boiling water in bottom of oven to create steam).
    Remove from oven and brush once more with olive oil before cooling.

Serves 6 · Preparation 2½ hours, plus standing time · Cooking 20 minutes

PIES & TARTS

What is a better cure for the winter blues (or a savoury treat the whole year round) than a meat pie and sauce? Savoury pies combine crispy and crumbly pastry with slow-cooked meat and silky gravy. Follow with a sweet tart, such as rhubarb and apple tart, raspberry and hazelnut tarts or fresh fruit tartlets, and you have the perfect two-course meal!

PEAR AND FIG FLAN

Hazelnut pastry
2 cups flour, sifted
45g/1½ oz finely chopped hazelnuts
1 teaspoon ground mixed spice
200g/7 oz butter, chilled and cut into small cubes
1 egg yolk, lightly beaten with a few drops vanilla extract

Pear and fig filling
4 pears, peeled, cored and quartered
90g/3 oz butter
125g/4 oz dried figs, chopped
½ cup brown sugar
½ cup golden (corn) syrup
½ teaspoon vanilla extract
½ cup plain (all-purpose) flour
1 egg, lightly beaten

1   Preheat oven to 220°C/430°F. To make pastry, place flour, hazelnuts and mixed spice in a bowl then, using fingertips, rub in butter until mixture resembles fine breadcrumbs. Using a metal spatula or round-ended knife, mix in egg yolk mixture and enough chilled water (3–4 tablespoons) to form a soft dough. Turn dough onto a lightly floured surface and knead gently until smooth. Wrap dough in plastic wrap and chill for 30 minutes.

2   On a lightly floured surface, roll out pastry and use to line a lightly buttered, deep 23cm/9 in flan tin. Chill for 15 minutes. Line pastry case with baking paper, fill with uncooked rice and bake for 10 minutes. Remove rice and paper and cook for 10 minutes more.

3   To make filling, cut each pear quarter into four slices. Melt 45g/1½ oz butter in a frying pan (skillet) over a medium heat, add pears and cook for 4–5 minutes. Arrange pear slices in pastry case, then scatter with figs.

4   Place remaining butter, sugar, golden (corn) syrup, ½ cup water and the vanilla in a saucepan and cook over a medium heat until sugar dissolves. Bring to the boil and simmer for 2 minutes.

5   Remove pan from heat and set aside to cool for 15 minutes, then beat in flour and egg. Pour mixture over pears and figs and bake at 180°C/360°F for 50–55 minutes or until filling is firm.

Serves 8 · Preparation 1 hour · Cooking 1½ hours

RHUBARB AND APPLE TART

Pastry
1 cup plain (all-purpose) flour, sifted
2 teaspoons icing (confectioner's) sugar, sifted
90g/3 oz butter, cubed

Rhubarb and apple filling
6 stalks rhubarb, chopped
2 tablespoons sugar
30g/1 oz butter
3 green apples, cored, peeled and sliced
125g/4 oz cream cheese
⅓ cup sugar
1 teaspoon vanilla extract
1 egg

1   Preheat oven to 200°C/400°F. To make pastry, place flour and icing (confectioner's) sugar in a bowl and rub in butter, using your fingertips, until mixture resembles coarse breadcrumbs. Add 4 teaspoons iced water and knead to a smooth dough. Wrap in plastic wrap and refrigerate for 30 minutes.

2   Roll out pastry on a lightly floured surface and line a buttered 23cm/9 in fluted flan tin with removable base. Line pastry case with non-stick baking paper and weigh down with uncooked rice. Bake for 15 minutes. Remove rice and paper and cook for 5 minutes longer.

3   To make filling, poach rhubarb until tender. Drain well, stir in sugar and set aside to cool. Melt butter in a frying pan (skillet) and cook apples for 3–4 minutes. Remove apples from pan and set aside to cool.

4   Place cream cheese, sugar, vanilla extract and egg in a bowl and beat until smooth. Spoon rhubarb into pastry case, then top with cream cheese mixture and arrange apple slices attractively on top. Reduce oven temperature to 180°C/360°F and cook for 40–45 minutes or until filling is firm.

Serves 10 • Preparation 45 minutes • Cooking 1 hour 15 minutes

RASPBERRY AND HAZELNUT TARTS

1 cup flour, sifted
2 tablespoons icing (confectioner's) sugar
30g/1 oz hazelnuts, ground
75g/2½ oz unsalted butter, chopped
1 egg, lightly beaten

Cream filling
375g/13 oz cream cheese
2 tablespoons caster (berry) sugar
¼ cup thickened (whipping) cream

Raspberry topping
350g/12 oz raspberries
⅓ cup raspberry jam (jelly), warmed and sieved

1   To make pastry, place flour, icing (confectioner's) sugar and hazelnuts in a bowl and mix to combine. Rub in butter, using fingertips, until mixture resembles fine breadcrumbs. Add egg and mix to form a soft dough. Wrap in plastic wrap and refrigerate for 1 hour.

2   Preheat oven to 200°C/400°F. Knead pastry lightly, then roll out to 3mm/⅛ in thick and line six lightly buttered 75mm/3 in flan tins. Line pastry cases with baking paper and weigh down with uncooked rice and bake for 10 minutes. Remove paper and rice and bake for 15 minutes longer or until golden. Set aside to cool.

3   To make filling, place cream cheese and sugar in a bowl and beat until smooth. Beat cream until soft peaks form then fold into cream cheese mixture. Cover and chill for 20 minutes.

4   To assemble, spoon filling into pastry cases and smooth tops. Arrange raspberries over top of tarts, then brush warm jam (jelly) over raspberries and refrigerate for a few minutes to set glaze.

Serves 6 • Preparation 40 minutes • Cooking 25 minutes

SPICY PUMPKIN PIE

Pastry
1 cup flour
½ teaspoon baking powder
100g/3½ oz butter, cut into pieces
1½ tablespoons caster (berry) sugar
1 egg yolk

Spicy pumpkin filling
300g/10½ oz pumpkin, cooked and puréed
2 eggs, lightly beaten
½ cup sour cream
½ cup thickened (whipping) cream
¼ cup golden (corn) syrup
½ teaspoon ground nutmeg
½ teaspoon ground mixed spice
½ teaspoon ground cinnamon

1 Preheat oven to 200°C/400°F.

2 To make pastry, sift flour and baking powder into a mixing bowl. Rub in butter with fingertips until mixture resembles coarse breadcrumbs, then stir in sugar. Make a well in the centre and mix in egg yolk and ½–1 tablespoon water to mix to a firm dough. Turn onto a floured surface and knead lightly until smooth. Wrap in plastic wrap and refrigerate for 30 minutes.

3 To make filling, place pumpkin, eggs, sour cream, cream, golden (corn) syrup, nutmeg, mixed spice and cinnamon in a mixing bowl and beat until smooth and well combined.

4 Roll pastry out and line a buttered 23cm/9 in flan tin with removable base. Spoon filling into pastry case. Bake for 20 minutes, then reduce heat to 160°C/320°F and bake for 25–30 minutes longer or until filling is set and pastry golden. Allow to stand in tin for 5 minutes before removing. Serve hot, warm or cold with whipped (double) cream.

Serves 8 • Preparation 45 minutes • Cooking 50 minutes

Fresh fruit tartlets

Sweet almond pastry
¼ cup plain (all-purpose) flour
¾ cups self-raising flour
⅓ cup cornflour (cornstarch)
⅓ cup ground almonds
¼ cup icing (confectioner's) sugar
150g/5 oz butter
1 egg yolk

Filling
100g/3½ oz ricotta cheese
¼ cup sugar
100g/3½ oz thickened (whipping) cream
¼ cup milk mixed with 1 tablespoon of arrowroot
½ cup cooked white short-grain rice or semolina
fruit for decorating (for example, blueberries, strawberries,
peaches, mangoes, kiwifruit)
¼ cup apple and blackcurrant baby jelly (dessert baby food) warmed

1   Preheat oven to 190°C/380°F. To make the pastry, combine flours, almonds and sugar in a bowl. Rub in butter until mixture resembles fine breadcrumbs. Stir in egg and enough iced water (about ¼ cup) to make ingredients just come together. Knead on a floured surface until smooth. Wrap in plastic wrap. Refrigerate for at least 30 minutes.

2   Roll out pastry to 3mm/⅛ in thick. Using a 75mm/3 in round fluted cutter, cut out 24 rounds. Gently ease pastry into buttered muffin or patty pans. Prick all over with a fork. Line with foil or baking paper. Weigh down with uncooked rice and bake for 10 minutes. Remove rice and foil. Bake for a further 5–6 minutes or until golden, then cool.

3   Mix ricotta cheese, sugar and cream until light and smooth. Combine ricotta mixture and milk mixture with rice or semolina in a saucepan. Cook, stirring, over medium heat for 5–10 minutes or until mixture starts to thicken. Cool. Divide mixture between pastry cases. Top with fruit. Brush with warmed jelly (dessert baby food). Chill until ready to serve.

Makes 24 · Preparation 50 minutes · Cooking 25 minutes

FRUIT PIES

Fruit filling
¼ cup mixed peel
¼ cup sultanas (golden raisins)
¼ cup raisins (dark raisins)
¼ cup currants
¼ cup chopped dried apricots
¼ cup drained, canned crushed
unsweetened pineapple
1 apple, finely chopped
2 tablespoons finely chopped almonds
or hazelnuts
1 teaspoon grated lemon zest
1 teaspoon grated orange zest
1 tablespoon orange juice

2 tablespoons brown sugar
1 teaspoon ground cloves
1 teaspoon ground cinnamon
1 teaspoon mixed spice
1 tablespoon rum

Sweet almond pastry
¼ cup plain (all-purpose) flour
¾ cups self-raising flour
⅓ cup cornflour (cornstarch)
⅓ cup ground almonds
¼ cup icing (confectioner's) sugar
150g/5 oz butter
1 egg, separated

1   To prepare the filling, place all ingredients in a bowl. Mix well. Place in an airtight container. Refrigerate for at least 5 days, turning occasionally.

2   To make the pastry, combine flours, almonds and sugar in a bowl. Rub in butter until mixture resembles fine breadcrumbs. Stir in egg yolk and enough iced water (about ¼ cup) to make ingredients just come together. Knead on a floured surface until smooth. Wrap in plastic wrap. Refrigerate for at least 30 minutes.

3   Preheat oven to 180°C/360°F.

4   Roll out pastry to 3mm/⅛ in thick. Cut pastry into 24 rounds, using a 75mm/3 in cutter. Cut remaining pastry into decorative shapes or rounds for top of pies.

5   Gently ease pastry rounds into buttered patty or muffin pans. Divide filling between pastry cases. Top with decorative pastry shapes. Brush pastry with egg white. Bake for 20–25 minutes or until golden.

Makes 24 · Preparation 30 minutes, plus standing time · Cooking 25 minutes

CORNISH PASTIES

1 egg, lightly beaten

Pastry
60g/2 oz butter, softened
60g/2 oz lard, softened
2 cups plain (all-purpose) flour, sifted

Beef and vegetable filling
250g/9 oz lean beef mince (ground beef)
1 small onion, grated
1 potato, peeled and grated
½ small turnip, peeled and grated
¼ cup fresh parsley, chopped
1 tablespoon Worcestershire sauce
freshly ground black pepper

1   Preheat oven to 220°C/430°F.
2   To make pastry, place butter and lard in a bowl and mix well to combine. Cover and refrigerate until firm. Place flour in a bowl. Chop butter mixture into small pieces and, using fingertips, rub into flour until mixture resembles coarse breadcrumbs. Mix in enough cold water (about ⅓ cup) to form a soft dough, then turn pastry onto a floured surface and knead lightly. Wrap in plastic wrap and chill for 30 minutes.
3   To make filling, place meat, onion, potato, turnip, parsley, Worcestershire sauce and black pepper to taste in a bowl and mix well to combine.
4   Roll out pastry on a lightly floured surface to 6mm/¼ in thick and, using an upturned saucer as a guide, cut out six 15cm/6 in rounds. Divide filling between pastry rounds. Brush edges with water and fold the pastry rounds in half upwards to enclose filling.
5   Press pastry edges together to seal, then flute between finger and thumb. Place pasties on a buttered baking tray (sheet), brush with egg and bake for 15 minutes. Reduce oven temperature to 160°C/320°F and bake for 20 minutes or until golden.

Makes 6 · Preparation 45 minutes · Cooking 35 minutes

INDIVIDUAL MEAT PIES

750g/1½ lb prepared shortcrust pastry
375g/13 oz prepared puff pastry
1 egg, lightly beaten

Beef filling
750g/1½ lb lean beef mince (ground beef)
2 cups beef stock (broth)
freshly ground black pepper
2 tablespoons cornflour (cornstarch), blended with ½ cup water
1 tablespoon Worcestershire sauce
1 teaspoon soy sauce

1 Preheat oven to 220°C/430°F.

2 To make filling, heat a frying pan (skillet) over a medium heat, add meat and cook until brown. Drain off juices, stir in stock (broth) and black pepper to taste and bring to the boil. Reduce heat, cover and simmer for 20 minutes. Stir in cornflour (cornstarch) mixture and Worcestershire and soy sauces and cook, stirring, until mixture boils and thickens. Cool.

3 Roll out shortcrust pastry to 5mm/⅕ in thick and use to line base and sides of eight buttered, small metal pie dishes. Roll out puff pastry to same thickness and cut out rounds to fit top of pies.

4 Divide filling between pie dishes. Brush edges of shortcrust pastry with water, top with rounds of puff pastry and press edges together to seal. Brush pies with egg and bake for 5 minutes, then reduce oven temperature to 180°C/360°F and bake for a further 10–15 minutes or until pastry is golden.

Makes 8 · Preparation 25 minutes · Cooking 45 minutes

BEEF AND MUSHROOM PIE

Puff Pastry
90g/30 oz butter, softened
90g/30 oz lard, softened
2 cups plain (all-purpose) flour

Beef and mushroom filling
1kg/2 lb lean beef, cut into 25mm/1 in cubes
¼ cup seasoned plain flour
90g/30 oz butter
3 tablespoons olive oil
2 onions, chopped

2 cloves garlic, crushed
2 cups sliced mushrooms
½ cup red wine
½ cup beef stock (broth)
1 bay leaf
¼ cup fresh parsley, finely chopped
1 tablespoon Worcestershire sauce
freshly ground black pepper
1 egg, lightly beaten

1   For the filling, toss meat in flour to coat. Shake off excess. Melt butter and oil in a large heavy-based saucepan and cook meat in batches for 3–4 minutes, or until browned. Remove meat from pan and set aside.

2   Add onions and garlic to pan and cook over medium heat for 3–4 minutes, or until softened. Stir in mushrooms and cook for 2 minutes longer. Combine the wine and stock (broth), pour into pan and cook for 4–5 minutes. Bring to the boil, then reduce heat. Return meat to the pan with bay leaf, parsley, Worcestershire sauce and pepper to taste. Cover and simmer for 1½ hours or until the meat is tender. Remove pan from the heat and set aside to cool.

3   For the pastry, mix butter and lard until well combined. Cover and refrigerate until firm. Place flour in a large mixing bowl. Cut butter mixture into small pieces and rub a quater into flour with your fingertips until mixture resembles breadcrumbs. Add enough cold water to form a firm dough (about ½ cup).

4   Turn pastry onto a floured surface and knead lightly. Roll to a 15 x 25cm/6 x 10 in rectangle. Place another quarter of butter mixture over top two-thirds of pastry. Fold bottom third of pastry up and top third down to give 3 even layers. Half turn to have the open end facing you, and roll to a rectangle as before. Repeat the folding and rolling twice, adding more butter mixture each time. Cover pastry and refrigerate 1 hour.

5   Preheat oven to 190°C/380°F. Place cooled filling in a 4-cup capacity pie dish. Roll out pastry 25mm/1 in larger than the pie dish. Cut off a 12mm/½ in strip from pastry edge. Brush the pastry strip with water. Lift the pastry top over the filling and press gently to seal the edges. Trim and knock back edges. Brush with egg and bake for 30 minutes or until the pastry is golden and crisp.

Serves 4 · Preparation 1 hour 30 minutes · Cooking 2 hours

POTATO, EGG AND LEEK PIES

500g/1 lb shortcrust pastry
1 egg, lightly beaten

Potato and leek filling
30g/1 oz butter
4 leeks, sliced
2 cloves garlic, crushed
2 teaspoons curry powder
6 potatoes, cooked until tender, chopped
300g/10½ oz asparagus, stalks removed, chopped and blanched
4 hard boiled eggs, chopped
125g/4 oz aged cheddar cheese, grated
¼ cup fresh parsley, chopped
⅔ cup sour cream
2 egg yolks, lightly beaten
freshly ground black pepper
1 egg, lightly beaten
caraway seeds

1 Preheat oven to 220°C/430°F.
2 To make filling, melt butter in a frying pan (skillet) over a low heat, add leeks and cook for 3–4 minutes or until soft. Increase heat to medium, stir in garlic and curry powder and cook for 1 minute. Combine potatoes, leek mixture, asparagus, chopped eggs, cheese, parsley, sour cream, egg yolks and black pepper to taste. Cool completely.
3 Roll out shortcrust pastry to 5mm/⅕ in thick cut to fit the base and sides of ten buttered, metal pie dishes. Cut remaining pastry to fit tops of pies. Spoon filling into pie dishes, brush pastry edges with egg and top with pie lids. Press pastry edges together to seal. Using a sharp knife, make a slit on the top of each pie, then brush with egg and bake for 15 minutes. Sprinkle with caraway seeds. Reduce oven temperature to 180°C/360°F and bake for 15 minutes or until golden.

Makes 10 pies • Preparation 25 minutes • Cooking 40 minutes

DESSERTS, CAKES & CHEESECAKES

It is curious that no matter how satisfied we are after a meal, our tastebuds tell us there is always room for something sweet. Our 'dessert' stomach becomes surprisingly barren in the face of creamy puddings, floaty soufflés, sumptuous cakes or the crumbly crust and cream-cheese filling of a cheesecake. For virtually any celebration – or for no reason at all – life would not be complete without these home-baked treats.

THE PERFECT PAVLOVA

6 egg whites
1½ cups caster (berry) sugar
6 teaspoons cornflour (cornstarch), sifted
1½ teaspoons white vinegar
315mL/11 fl oz thickened (whipping) cream, whipped
selection of fresh fruits, such as orange segments,
sliced bananas, sliced peaches, passionfruit pulp, berries or sliced kiwifruit

1   Preheat oven to 120°C/250°F.

2   Place egg whites in a mixing bowl and beat until soft peaks form. Gradually add
    sugar, beating well after each addition, until mixture is thick and glossy.

3   Fold cornflour (cornstarch) and vinegar into egg white mixture. Butter a baking
    tray (sheet) and line with non-stick baking paper. Butter paper and dust lightly with
    flour. Mark a 23cm/9 in diameter circle on paper.

4   Place the egg white mixture in the centre of the circle and spread out to within
    edge of circle and neaten using a metal spatula or knife. Bake for 1½–2 hours
    or until firm to touch. Turn off oven and cool pavlova in oven with door ajar.
    Decorate cold pavlova with cream and top with fruit.

Serves 8 • Preparation 25 minutes • Cooking 2 hours

APPLE AND RHUBARB CRUMBLE

8 stalks rhubarb, cut into 5cm/2 in pieces
4 cooking apples, cored, peeled and sliced
½ cup caster (berry) sugar
¼ cup orange juice

Hazelnut crumble
½ cup ground hazelnuts
½ cup rolled oats
⅓ cup plain (all-purpose) flour
¼ cup brown sugar
3 tablespoons desiccated (fine) coconut
¼ teaspoon ground cinnamon
90g/3 oz butter, chopped into small pieces

1   Preheat oven to 180°C/360°F.
2   Place rhubarb, apples, caster (berry) sugar, ½ cup water and the orange juice in a saucepan and cook, stirring constantly, over a medium heat, until sugar dissolves. Bring to the boil, then reduce heat, cover and simmer for 10 minutes or until fruit is tender. Spoon fruit mixture into a 3-cup capacity ovenproof dish.
3   To make crumble, place hazelnuts, oats, flour, brown sugar, coconut and cinnamon in a bowl and mix to combine. Using fingertips, rub in butter until mixture resembles coarse breadcrumbs. Sprinkle crumble over fruit mixture and bake for 20–25 minutes.

Serves 4 • Preparation 20 minutes • Cooking 35 minutes

PEAR UPSIDE DOWN PUDDING

¼ cup demerara sugar
825g/29 oz canned pear halves, drained and 1 cup syrup reserved
250g/9 oz butter, softened
2 cups self-raising flour
1 cup caster (berry) sugar
4 eggs
1 cup chopped walnuts
¼ cup maple syrup

1   Preheat oven to 180°C/360°F.

2   Sprinkle base of a buttered and lined, deep 23cm/9 in round cake tin with demerara sugar. Cut pear halves in half to form quarters and arrange cut-side up, over base.

3   Place butter, flour, sugar and eggs in a food processor and process until smooth. Stir in walnuts. Carefully spoon batter over fruit in tin and bake for 1–1¼ hours or until cooked when tested with a skewer.

4   Place maple syrup and reserved pear juice in a saucepan over a medium heat and cook until syrup is reduced by half.

5   Turn pudding onto a serving plate and pour over syrup. Serve with cream or ice-cream.

Serves 8 · Preparation 20 minutes · Cooking 1 hour 15 minutes

CITRUS DELICIOUS PUDDING

1 cup caster (berry) sugar
125g/4 oz butter, softened
½ cup self-raising flour
1 tablespoon finely grated lemon zest
1 tablespoon finely grated orange zest
2 tablespoons lemon juice
2 tablespoons orange juice
2 eggs, separated
1 cup milk

1   Preheat oven to 180°C/360°F.
2   Place sugar and butter in a bowl and beat until light and fluffy. Stir in flour, lemon and orange zests and lemon and orange juices.
3   Place egg yolks and milk in a bowl and whisk to combine. Stir into citrus mixture.
4   Place egg whites in a bowl and beat until stiff peaks form, then fold into batter. Spoon batter into a buttered 4-cup capacity ovenproof dish. Place dish in a baking pan with enough boiling water to come halfway up the sides of dish. Bake for 45 minutes or until cooked.

Serves 6 • Preparation 20 minutes • Cooking 45 minutes

ORANGE LIQUEUR SOUFFLÉ

½ cup orange juice
1 teaspoon grated orange zest
¾ cup cooked long-grain rice
4 egg yolks
1 tablespoon caster (berry) sugar, plus ⅓ cup extra
1 tablespoon cornflour (cornstarch)
1¼ cups milk
4 tablespoons orange liqueur
5 egg whites

1   Preheat oven to 220°C/430°F.

2   Place orange juice, zest and rice in a saucepan and bring to the boil. Reduce heat and allow to simmer, stirring occasionally until all liquid has been absorbed. Set aside.

3   Whisk together egg yolks, 1 tablespoon caster (berry) sugar and cornflour (cornstarch). Heat milk in a saucepan until just at boiling point. Add to egg yolk mixture, whisk, then return mixture to saucepan. Stir over medium heat until custard boils and thickens. Reduce heat and simmer for 3–4 minutes, stirring constantly. Remove from heat. Stir in orange liqueur and rice mixture. Cool slightly.

4   Beat egg whites until stiff peaks form. Add extra sugar, a tablespoon at a time, beating after each addition. Stir a little beaten egg white into rice custard then lightly fold in remaining whites. Spoon into prepared soufflé dish. Bake for 20–25 minutes until soufflé is puffed and golden. Serve immediately.

Serves 4 • Preparation 30 minutes • Cooking 40 minutes

RASPBERRY CHOCOLATE TRUFFLE CAKES

½ cup cocoa powder, sifted
125g/4 oz butter
1¾ cups caster (berry) sugar
2 eggs
1⅔ cups self-raising flour, sifted
400g/14 oz dark (semi-sweet) chocolate, melted
fresh raspberries

Raspberry cream
125g/4 oz raspberries, puréed and sieved
½ cup thickened (whipping) cream, whipped
fresh raspberries to serve

1 Preheat oven to 180°C/360°F.

2 Combine cocoa powder and 1 cup boiling water. Mix to dissolve and set aside to cool.

3 Place butter and sugar in a bowl and beat until light and fluffy. Beat in eggs, one at a time, adding a little flour with each egg. Fold remaining flour and cocoa mixture, alternately, into creamed butter mixture.

4 Spoon mixture into eight lightly buttered ½-cup capacity ramekins or large muffin tins. Bake for 20–25 minutes or until cakes are cooked when tested with a skewer. Cool for 5 minutes, then turn onto wire racks to cool. Turn cakes upside down and scoop out centre, leaving a 12mm/½ in shell. Spread each cake with chocolate to cover top and sides, then place right way up on a wire rack.

5 To make cream, fold raspberry purée into cream. Spoon cream into a piping bag fitted with a large nozzle. Carefully turn cakes upside down and pipe in cream to fill cavity. Place right way up on individual serving plates. Garnish with fresh raspberries.

Serves 8 · Preparation 25 minutes · Cooking 25 minutes

SPICED APPLE CAKE

2 apples, cored, peeled and sliced
125g/4 oz butter
1 cup raw or demerara sugar
2 eggs
1 cup self-raising flour
1 cup wholemeal (whole wheat) flour
½ teaspoon bicarbonate of soda (baking soda)
1½ teaspoons ground mixed spice
30g/1 oz walnuts, chopped
60g/2 oz raisins (dark raisins), chopped
¾ cup thickened (whipping) cream, whipped
icing (confectioner's) sugar, sifted

1   Preheat oven to 180°C/360°F.

2   Place apples and ¾ cup water in a saucepan and cook over a medium heat until tender. Place in a food processor or blender and process until smooth. Set aside to cool.

3   Place butter and sugar in a bowl and beat until light and fluffy. Add eggs, one at a time, beating well after each addition.

4   Sift together self-raising flour, wholemeal (whole wheat) flour, bicarbonate of soda (baking soda) and 1 teaspoon of the mixed spice into a bowl. Return husks to bowl. Mix flour mixture and apple mixture, alternately, into butter mixture, then stir in walnuts and raisins (dark raisins).

5   Spoon batter into a buttered and lined 23cm/9 in round cake tin and bake for 40 minutes or until cooked when tested with a skewer. Allow to cool in tin for 5 minutes before turning onto a wire rack to cool completely.

6   Split cake in half horizontally, spread bottom half with cream, then top with other half and dust with remaining mixed spice and icing (confectioner's) sugar.

Makes one cake • Preparation 20 minutes • Cooking 50 minutes

ORANGE POPPY SEED CAKE

4 tablespoons poppy seeds
¼ cup orange juice
125g/4 oz natural yoghurt
200g/7 oz butter, softened
1 tablespoon finely grated orange zest
1 cup caster (berry) sugar
3 eggs
2 cups self-raising flour, sifted
2 tablespoons orange marmalade, warmed

1   Preheat oven to 180°C/360°F.

2   Place poppy seeds, orange juice and yoghurt into a bowl, mix to combine and set aside to stand for 1 hour.

3   Place butter and orange zest in a bowl and beat until light and fluffy. Gradually add sugar, beating well after each addition until mixture is creamy.

4   Add eggs one at a time, beating well after each addition. Fold flour and poppy seed mixture, alternately, into butter mixture.

5   Spoon batter into a buttered 20cm/8 in fluted ring tin and bake for 35–40 minutes or until cooked when tested with a skewer. Stand in tin for 5 minutes before turning onto a wire rack to cool completely. Brush with orange marmalade before serving.

Makes one cake • Preparation 1 hour 20 minutes • Cooking 40 minutes

PECAN AND ALMOND CAKES

2 eggs, separated
½ cup caster (berry) sugar
few drops of vanilla extract
½ cup plain (all-purpose) flour
1 teaspoon baking powder
¼ cup mixed pecans and almonds, chopped
2 tablespoons icing (confectioner's) sugar

1   Preheat oven to 150°C/300°F.

2   Butter 12 individual bun tins. Whisk egg yolks with sugar until thick and pale.
    Gently stir in vanilla. Sift together flour and baking powder over surface of egg yolk
    mixture, then fold in.

3   In a clean bowl, whisk egg whites until stiff then fold gently into egg yolk mixture.
    Carefully fold nuts into mixture. Divide among prepared bun tins and bake for
    15 minutes. Sieve icing (confectioner's) sugar over and serve warm.

Makes 12 · Preparation 20 minutes · Cooking 15 minutes

VICTORIA SANDWICH CAKE

4 eggs
¾ cup caster (berry) sugar
1 cup self-raising flour
1 tablespoon cornflour (cornstarch)
1½ teaspoons melted butter
1 tablespoon icing (confectioner's) sugar, sifted

Filling
½ cup strawberry jam (jelly)
½ cup thickened (whipping) cream, whipped

1   Preheat oven to 180°C/360°F.

2   Place eggs in a bowl and beat until thick and creamy. Gradually beat in caster (berry) sugar and continue beating until mixture becomes thick. This will take about 10 minutes.

3   Sift flour and cornflour (cornstarch) together over egg mixture, then fold in. Stir in ⅓ cup warm water and the melted butter.

4   Divide mixture evenly between two buttered and lined 20cm/8 in round sandwich tins.

5   Bake for 20–25 minutes or until cakes shrink slightly from sides of tins and spring back when touched with the fingertips. Stand cakes in tins for 5 minutes before turning onto wire racks to cool.

6   To assemble, spread one cake with jam (jelly), then top with whipped cream and remaining sponge cake. Just prior to serving, dust cake with icing (confectioner's) sugar.

Makes one cake • Preparation 30 minutes • Cooking 25 minutes

ORANGE AND LIME CHEESECAKE

1 cup plain sweet biscuits (cookies), crushed
60g/2 oz butter, melted
shredded (medium) coconut, toasted

Orange and lime filling
250g/9 oz cream cheese, softened
2 tablespoons brown sugar
1½ teaspoons finely grated orange zest
1½ teaspoons finely grated lime zest
3 teaspoons orange juice
3 teaspoons lime juice
1 egg, lightly beaten
½ cup sweetened condensed milk
2 tablespoons thickened (whipping) cream, whipped

1   Preheat oven to 180°C/360°F.

2   Place the biscuits (cookies) and butter in a bowl and mix to combine. Press the biscuit mixture over the base and up the sides of a well-buttered 23cm/9 in flan tin with a removable base. Bake for 5–8 minutes, then cool.

3   To make the orange and lime filling, place the cream cheese, sugar, orange and lime zests and juices in a bowl and beat until creamy. Beat in the egg, then mix in the condensed milk and fold in the cream.

4   Spoon the filling into the prepared biscuit case and bake for 25–30 minutes or until just firm. Turn the oven off and cool the cheesecake in the oven with the door ajar. Chill before serving. Serve decorated with the toasted coconut.

Serves 8 · Preparation 30 minutes · Cooking 40 minutes

CHOCOLATE CARAMEL CHEESECAKE

Base
150g/5 oz shredded wheatmeal biscuits
(digestive biscuits/graham crackers),
finely crushed
60g/2 oz butter, melted

Filling
¼ cup evaporated milk
400g/14 oz canned caramel
1 cup pecans, chopped

500g/1 lb cream cheese
½ cup sugar
2 eggs
1 teaspoon vanilla extract
¾ cup chocolate chips, melted

Decorations
flaky chocolate bar jersey caramels
whipped (double) cream

1   Preheat oven to 180°C/360°F.

2   To make the base, combine crumbs and melted butter. Press mixture evenly into a
23cm/9 in springform tin. Bake for 8 minutes. Remove from oven and allow to cool.

3   To make the filling, combine milk and caramel in a heavy-based saucepan. Cook
over low heat until melted, stirring often. Pour over biscuit base. Sprinkle pecans
evenly over caramel layer and set aside.

4   Beat cream cheese at high speed with electric mixer until light and fluffy. Gradually
add sugar, mixing well. Add eggs one at a time, beating well after each addition.
Stir in vanilla and melted chocolate, beat until blended. Pour over pecan layer.

5   Bake for 30 minutes. Remove from oven and run knife around edge of tin to
release sides. Cool to room temperature. Cover and chill for 8 hours.

6   Decorate with a chopped flaky chocolate bar and chopped jersey caramels. Serve
with whipped (double) cream.

Makes 12 slices · Preparation 30 minutes, plus standing time · Cooking 40 minutes

FRUIT AND BOURBON CHEESECAKE

Base
60g/2 oz shredded wheatmeal biscuits (digestive biscuits/graham crackers),
finely crushed
30g/1 oz butter, melted
¼ cup sugar

Filling
1½ cups sultanas (golden raisins)
¼ cup bourbon
500g/1 lb cream cheese, softened
¼ cup sugar
1 tablespoon lemon juice
zest of ½ lemon
2 large eggs

1   Preheat oven to 165°C/330°F.

2   Soak the sultanas (golden raisins) in the bourbon for at least 2 hours.

3   To make the base, combine crumbs, butter and sugar. Line four 10cm/4 in springform tins with baking paper, then press mixture evenly onto bottoms of tins. Bake for 5 minutes.

4   To make the filling, combine cream cheese, sugar, juice and zest in an electric mixer, mix on medium speed until well blended. Add eggs one at a time, mixing thoroughly between additions. Chop 1 cup of the soaked sultanas roughly and add to the filling, then divide filling evenly between tins.

5   Bake for 25 minutes. Cool before removing from tins, then chill.

6   Let stand at room temperature for minimum of 40 minutes. Decorate with the remaining sultanas and serve with whipped (double) cream if desired.

Serves 4 · Preparation 30 minutes, plus standing time · Cooking 30 minutes

Hazelnut raspberry cheesecake

200g/7 oz ameretti biscuits (cookies), finely crushed
60g/2 oz butter, melted

Filling
1kg/2 lb cream cheese, softened
1¼ cups sugar
3 large eggs
1 cup sour cream
1 teaspoon vanilla extract
170g/6 oz hazelnut spread
⅓ cup raspberry jam (jelly)

1   Preheat oven to 165°C/330°F.
2   To make the base, combine crumbs and butter, press onto bottom of a 23cm/9 in springform tin.
3   To make the filling, combine three-quarters of the cream cheese with the sugar in an electric mixer and mix on medium speed until well blended. Add eggs one at a time, beating well after each addition. Blend in sour cream and vanilla, then pour over base.
4   Combine remaining cream cheese and the hazelnut spread in the electric mixer, mix on medium speed until well blended. Add raspberry jam (jelly), mix well.
5   Drop heaped tablespoonfuls of hazelnut mixture into plain cream cheese filling – do not swirl.
6   Bake for 1 hour and 25 minutes. Loosen cake from rim of tin, cool before removing. Serve with fresh raspberries.

Makes 12 slices • Preparation 30 minutes • Cooking 1 hour 25 minutes

Mini passionfruit cheesecakes

Base
60g/2 oz shredded wheatmeal biscuits (digestive biscuits/graham crackers), finely crushed
30g/1 oz butter, melted
¼ cup sugar

Filling
500g/1 lb cream cheese, softened
¼ cup passionfruit pulp, strained
1 teaspoon vanilla extract
¼ cup sugar
2 large eggs
4 fresh passionfruit

1 Preheat oven to 165°C/330°F.
2 To make the base, combine crumbs, butter and sugar. Line four 10cm/4 in springform tins with baking paper, then press mixture evenly onto bottoms of tins. Bake for 5 minutes.
3 To make the filling, combine cream cheese, passionfruit pulp, vanilla and sugar in an electric mixer, mix on medium speed until well combined. Add the eggs one at a time, mixing well after each addition. Divide filling evenly between the bases.
4 Bake for 25 minutes. Cool before removing from tins.
5 Decorate with fresh passionfruit and serve.

Serves 4 • Preparation 30 minutes • Cooking 30 minutes

TOFFEE CHEESECAKE

Base
100g/3½ oz vanilla wafers, finely crushed
90g/3 oz butter, melted

Filling
400g/14 oz soft caramel sweets
1 cup dark (semi-sweet) chocolate chips
½ cup evaporated milk
3 chocolate bars covered in toffee,
40g/1.4 oz each

1kg/2 lb cream cheese
1½ cups sugar
2 tablespoons plain (all-purpose) flour
4 whole eggs
2 egg yolks
⅓ cup whipped (double) cream

Topping
whipped (double) cream
chocolate caramel sweets

1   Preheat oven to 175°C/350°F.

2   To make the base, combine wafer crumbs with the melted butter in a medium-size
    bowl. Mix well. Press onto bottom and sides of a 23cm/9 in springform tin. Bake
    for 10 minutes, remove and allow to cool.

3   To make the filling, increase oven temperature to 200°C/400°F. In a saucepan
    over low heat, melt caramels together with the chocolate chips and evaporated
    milk, stir until smooth and pour into base. Break the chocolate bars into small
    pieces and sprinkle over the caramel layer.

4   Beat cream cheese until smooth. Add sugar and 2 tablespoons flour and beat until
    smooth. Add whole eggs and egg yolks one at a time, mixing well after each
    addition. Blend in cream, then pour over caramel and toffee layers. Wrap outside
    of pan with foil.

5   Set in a large pan that has been filled with 12mm/½ in of hot water. Bake for
    15 minutes, reduce oven to 110°C/230°F and bake for another hour. Remove from
    water, cool to room temperature then chill overnight in the refrigerator.

6   Top with whipped (double) cream and chocolate caramel sweets to serve.

Makes 12 slices • Preparation 40 minutes, plus standing time
• Cooking 1 hour 30 minutes

PLUM AND BITTER ORANGE CHEESECAKE

Base
150g/5 oz gingernut biscuits (cookies)
90g/3 oz butter, melted

Filling
825g/29 oz canned plums in juice
500g/1 lb cream cheese, softened
½ cup sour cream
zest of ½ orange
1 tablespoon orange juice
2–3 drops bitters
3 eggs

¾ cup caster (berry) sugar
2 tablespoons plain (all-purpose) flour
2 tablespoons flaked almonds

Topping
¼ cup caster (berry) sugar
¼ cup unsweetened orange juice
zest of 1 orange
3–4 drops bitters
½ cup thickened (whipping) cream
2 teaspoons ground cinnamon

1   Preheat oven to 150°C/300°F.

2   To make the base, line base of a 23cm/9 in springform tin with baking paper.
    In a food processor, process the biscuits (cookies) until finely crushed, transfer to a
    bowl and stir in the melted butter until combined. Press firmly over the base of the
    tin and refrigerate while preparing filling.

3   To make the filling, drain the plums, reserving the liquid. Halve the plums and
    remove any stones.

4   Combine the remaining filling ingredients, except the almonds, in a large bowl.
    Beat with an electric mixer for about 5 minutes or until thick and smooth.

5   Pour filling over the base, top with the plums and sprinkle with almonds.
    Bake, uncovered, for 1 hour or until set. Cool in the tin.

6   To make the topping, place the reserved plum juice with the sugar, juice, zest and
    bitters in a small saucepan, bring to the boil, then simmer, uncovered, until reduced
    by half. Allow to cool.

7   Combine cream and cinnamon in a bowl and whisk to firm peaks.

8   Serve the cheesecake topped with the plum syrup and cinnamon cream.

Makes 12 slices • Preparation 30 minutes • Cooking 1 hour

COOKIES, SLICES & SQUARES

Cookies, slices and squares are the perfect accompaniment to a cup of coffee or tea. Also called biscuits, biscotti and a range of other names, cookies are also the classic after-school treat. Slices and squares are baked flat like cookies, but have the moistness of a cake. With delights such as cinnamon cookies, coconut-sprinkled lamingtons and Turkish baklava, there is a cookie, slice or square to please all tastes.

CINNAMON COOKIES

250g/9 oz soft butter
125g/4 oz caster (berry) sugar
1 teaspoon vanilla extract
3 cups plain (all-purpose) flour
2 teaspoons ground cinnamon
salt
1½ cups icing (confectioner's) sugar

1   Butter two baking trays (sheets). Beat together butter, sugar and vanilla extract.
    Stir in flour, 1 teaspoon cinnamon and a pinch of salt to make a soft dough. Cover
    and refrigerate for 1 hour.

2   Preheat oven to 180°C/360°F. Form mixture into 25mm/1 in balls and place on
    a prepared baking tray, leaving space between each one. Bake for 15 minutes.
    Remove from oven, leave on baking trays for a few minutes, then transfer to a wire
    rack to cool. Mix together icing (confectioner's) sugar and remaining cinnamon and
    sieve over the cookies before serving.

Makes 24 · Preparation 1 hour · Cooking 15 minutes

PECAN CRISPIES

3 egg whites
pinch of salt
1 teaspoon vanilla extract
¾ cup caster (berry) sugar
2 cups pecans, chopped

1   Preheat oven to 180°C/360°F.
2   Beat egg whites in a large bowl with an electric mixer until soft peaks form.
3   Add salt, vanilla and sugar, beat for a further 1 minute then fold in nuts.
4   Drop teaspoonfuls of mixture onto a baking-paper-lined baking tray (sheet).
5   Bake for 2–3 minutes, turn off oven and leave cookies in oven for 60 minutes.
6   Use a spatula to ease cookies off paper, store in an airtight container.

Makes about 72 · Preparation 15 minutes · Cooking 3 minutes, plus standing time

OATMEAL COOKIES

125g/4 oz butter
1 cup brown sugar
2 eggs
2 ripe bananas, mashed
3 teaspoons vanilla extract
2½ cups plain (all-purpose) flour
1½ cups rolled oats
½ teaspoon baking powder
½ cup chopped hazelnuts

1 Preheat oven to 180°C/360°F.
2 Cream butter and sugar using an electric mixer until fluffy. Add egg and beat well.
   Add banana and vanilla.
3 Combine flour, oats and baking powder in another bowl. Gradually, add the flour
   mixture and milk to banana mixture. Add hazelnuts.
4 Place tablespoons of mixture onto lightly buttered oven tray (sheet). Bake for
   10 minutes or until slightly browned on edges. Cool on wire rack.

Makes about 40 · Preparation 20 minutes · Cooking 10 minutes

ALMOND BISCOTTI

1⅔ cups plain (all-purpose) flour
½ teaspoon baking powder
2 large eggs
½ cup caster (berry) sugar
1 teaspoon vanilla extract
1 teaspoon grated orange zest
¾ cup blanched almonds, lightly toasted
egg white

1   Preheat oven to 180°C/360°F.
2   Sift flour and baking powder into a bowl. In a separate bowl, beat eggs, sugar, vanilla extract and orange zest until thick and creamy. Fold egg mixture and almonds into flour mixture.
3   Knead on a floured surface to a firm dough. Divide dough in half. Shape each piece into a log about 50mm/2 in wide and 25mm/1 in thick. Place on a buttered and floured baking tray (sheet). Brush with egg white.
4   Bake for 30 minutes or until firm. Cool for 10 minutes. Cut each log diagonally into 10mm/⅖ in thick slices. Place on baking trays. Bake for 20–30 minutes or until dry and crisp. Cool on wire racks. Store in an airtight container.

Makes 30 slices • Preparation 20 minutes • Cooking 1 hour

Peanut Butter and Honey Cookies

¾ cup crunchy peanut butter
⅔ cup honey
1 egg, lightly beaten
1 cup plain (all-purpose) flour, sifted
½ cup rolled oats
⅓ cup sultanas (golden raisins)

1   Preheat oven to 160°C/320°F.
2   Place peanut butter and honey in a saucepan. Cook, stirring, over low heat until soft and combined. Cool slightly. Stir in egg. Fold in remaining ingredients.
3   Shape teaspoons of mixture into balls. Place on paper-lined baking trays (sheets). Press lightly with a fork. Bake for 12 minutes or until golden. Cool on wire racks.

Makes 30 · Preparation 15 minutes · Cooking 12 minutes

GINGER COOKIES

30g/1 oz butter
¼ cup sugar
1 egg
½ cup wholemeal (whole wheat) plain (all-purpose) flour, sifted
½ cup white plain (all-purpose) flour, sifted
2 teaspoons ground ginger
1 tablespoon glacé (glazed) ginger
½ teaspoon ground nutmeg
¼ teaspoon ground cloves
2 tablespoons treacle (molasses) or golden (corn) syrup, warmed

1   Preheat oven to 160°C/320°F. Beat butter and sugar in a bowl until light and fluffy. Beat in egg. Stir in remaining ingredients. Cover and refrigerate for 1 hour.

2   Roll teaspoons of mixture into balls. Place on lightly buttered baking trays (sheets). Flatten slightly. Bake for 10–12 minutes or until golden.

Makes 28 · Preparation 1 hour · Cooking 12 minutes

GINGER SNAPS

1 cup brown sugar
3 teaspoons ground ginger
2 cups plain (all-purpose) flour
90g/3 oz butter
1 cup golden (corn) syrup
1 teaspoon baking powder

1   Preheat the oven to 180°C/360°F.

2   Sift the sugar, ginger and flour together into a bowl.

3   Place the butter and golden (corn) syrup in a saucepan and cook over a low heat, stirring, until the butter melts. Stir in the baking powder. Pour the syrup mixture into the dry ingredients and mix until smooth.

4   Drop teaspoons of the mixture onto buttered baking trays (sheets) and bake for 10–12 minutes or until golden. Remove from the oven, loosen the cookies with a spatula, and allow to cool on trays.

Makes 45 · Preparation 20 minutes · Cooking 12 minutes

CARAMEL SQUARES

Shortbread base
100g/3½ oz butter
3 tablespoons sugar
60g/2 oz cornflour (cornstarch), sifted
¾ cup plain (all-purpose) flour, sifted

Caramel filling
125g/4 oz butter
½ cup brown sugar
2 tablespoons honey
400g/14 oz sweetened condensed milk
1 teaspoon vanilla extract

Chocolate topping
200g/7 oz dark (semi-sweet) chocolate, melted

1 Preheat oven to 180°C/360°F. To make base, place butter and sugar in a bowl and beat until light and fluffy. Mix in cornflour (cornstarch) and flour, turn onto a lightly floured surface and knead briefly, then press into a buttered and lined 20 x 30cm/8 x 12 in shallow cake tin and bake for 25 minutes or until firm.

2 To make filling, place butter, brown sugar and honey in a saucepan and cook over a medium heat, stirring constantly until sugar melts and ingredients are combined. Bring to the boil and simmer for 7 minutes. Beat in condensed milk and vanilla extract, pour filling over base and bake for 20 minutes longer. Set aside to cool completely. Spread melted chocolate over filling, set aside until firm, then cut into squares.

Makes 25 · Preparation 25 minutes · Cooking 45 minutes

CHOCOLATE RUM SLICE

1 cup self-raising flour, sifted
1 tablespoon cocoa powder, sifted
½ cup caster (berry) sugar
75g/2½ oz desiccated (fine) coconut
75g/2½ oz raisins (dark raisins), chopped
125g/4 oz butter, melted
1 teaspoon rum
2 tablespoons grated dark (semi-sweet) chocolate
2 eggs, lightly beaten

Chocolate icing (frosting)
1 cup icing (confectioner's) sugar
2 tablespoons cocoa powder
15g/½ oz butter, softened
extra coconut

1 Preheat oven to 180°C/360°F. Place flour, cocoa powder, caster (berry) sugar, coconut and raisins (dark raisins) in a bowl and mix to combine. Stir in butter, rum, grated chocolate and eggs. Mix well.

2 Press mixture into a buttered and lined 25cm/10 in square cake tin and bake for 20–25 minutes or until firm. Allow to cool in tin.

3 To make icing (frosting), sift icing (confectioner's) sugar and cocoa powder together into a bowl. Add butter and 1 tablespoon boiling water and beat to make icing of a spreadable consistency.

4 Turn slice onto a wire rack or plate, spread with icing and sprinkle with extra coconut. Refrigerate until icing is firm, then cut into squares.

Makes 25 · Preparation 15 minutes · Cooking 25 minutes

BLUEBERRY PECAN LOAF

1 cup wholemeal (whole wheat) plain (all-purpose) flour
1 cup white plain (all-purpose) flour
1½ teaspoons baking powder
1 teaspoon salt
½ teaspoon bicarbonate of soda (baking soda)
45g/1½ oz butter
¾ cup natural yoghurt
1 tablespoon grated lemon zest
2 eggs
1 cup blueberries
1 cup chopped pecans

1   Preheat oven to 180°C/360°F.
2   Sift flours, baking powder, salt and bicarbonate of soda (baking soda) into a processor. Add butter, process until mixture resembles course breadcrumbs.
3   Combine yoghurt, zest and eggs in a separate bowl, mix well. Add to processor and process just long enough to moisten. Add blueberries and nuts, process just long enough to combine.
4   Spoon into a buttered loaf pan, bake for about 1 hour or until a skewer comes out clean. Cool on a cake rack. Turn out and cut into 12mm/½ in slices.

Makes about 18 slices • Preparation 20 minutes • Cooking 1 hour

CINNAMON NUT CIGARS

¼ cup walnuts, roughly chopped
1 tablespoon brown sugar
2 teaspoons ground cinnamon
6 sheets filo pastry
2 tablespoons light olive or canola oil
¼ cup pine nuts
egg white

1   Preheat oven to 180°C/360°F. Combine walnuts, sugar and cinnamon in a bowl. Layer two sheets of pastry with short side facing you. Lightly brush lower half of pastry with oil. Sprinkle with one-third of the nut mixture. Fold pastry in half. Lightly brush with oil. Sprinkle with one-third of the pine nuts. Cut into three strips lengthwise, then cut each strip in half. Roll up. Place seam side down on a buttered baking tray (sheet). Lightly brush with egg white. Repeat with remaining pastry, nut mixture and pine nuts.

2   Bake for 10–12 minutes or until golden. Cool on a wire rack.

Makes 36 · Preparation 30 minutes · Cooking 12 minutes

WALNUT CHOCOLATE SLICE

4 egg whites
¼ cup sugar
125g/4 oz chocolate, melted and cooled
90g/3 oz butter, melted and cooled
1½ teaspoons vanilla extract
1 cup plain (all-purpose) flour
¼ cup brown sugar
⅓ cup cocoa powder
2 teaspoons baking powder
½ teaspoon bicarbonate of soda (baking soda)
⅓ cup chopped walnuts or pecans

1   Preheat oven to 190°C/380°F. Beat egg whites until soft peaks form. Gradually
    beat in sugar. Beat until sugar dissolves. Fold in chocolate, butter and
    vanilla extract.

2   Sift flour, brown sugar, cocoa, baking powder and bicarbonate of soda (baking
    soda) into a large bowl. Make a well in the centre. Fold in egg whites and walnuts
    until just combined. Spoon into a buttered and lined 23cm/9 in square slab pan.

3   Bake for 20–25 minutes or until cooked when tested with a skewer. Cool in pan.
    Cut into 4–5cm/1½–2 in squares. Serve with fresh berries if desired.

Makes 25 • Preparation 20 minutes • Cooking 25 minutes

Perfect lamingtons

3 eggs
¾ cup caster (berry) sugar
¾ cup self-raising flour, sifted
¼ cup cornflour (cornstarch)
15g/½ oz butter

Chocolate icing (frosting)
2 cups icing (confectioner's) sugar, sifted
3 tablespoons cocoa powder
20g/¾ oz butter
2 cups shredded (medium) coconut

1   Preheat oven to 200°C/400°F.

2   Beat eggs until light with an electric mixer. Add sugar and beat until mixture is thick and creamy. Fold in sifted flours. Combine butter and 3 tablespoons boiling water and stir quickly and lightly into flour mixture.

3   Pour into a lightly buttered 18 x 28cm/7 x 11 in lamington tin (slice pan) and then bake for about 20 minutes.

4   Turn onto a cake stand to cool. Place in the freezer until firm but not solid. The lamingtons will cut and coat easier if half frozen.

5   Sift icing (confectioner's) sugar and cocoa into a bowl. Blend in butter and add 4 tablespoons boiling water, mix well until smooth. Stand bowl in a pan of boiling water and stir until running consistency. Leave bowl in hot water while dipping lamingtons to keep icing (frosting) the same consistency.

6   Place coconut on a sheet of paper on a flat surface.

7   Cut half-frozen cake into 12 even pieces. Hold each piece on a fork and quickly dip into warm icing, drain and toss into coconut to coat evenly. Place on a wire rack to set. Repeat with remainder.

Makes about 12 • Preparation 20 minutes • Cooking 20 minutes

BAKLAVA

250g/9 oz unsalted butter
400g/14 oz blanched roasted almonds, ground
1½ teaspoons ground cinnamon
½ cup caster (berry) sugar
700g/25 oz filo pastry

Syrup
3 cups caster (berry) sugar
1 cinnamon stick
1 piece of orange or lemon rind
1 tablespoon honey

1 Preheat oven to 275°C/530°F. Melt butter, set aside. Mix nuts in a bowl with cinnamon and sugar.

2 Brush a 25 x 33cm/10 x 13 in baking tray (sheet) with the butter.

3 Place one sheet of pastry on bottom of dish with ends hanging over sides. Brush with melted butter and add another layer of pastry. Repeat with 8 more pastry sheets.

4 Sprinkle nut mixture generously over the pastry. Continue layering 3 sheets of pastry and one layer of nuts until all nuts are used.

5 Top with 8 sheets of pastry, making sure the top sheet is well buttered. Cut the top lengthwise in parallel strips.

6 Bake for 30 minutes, then reduce heat to 150°C/300°F and bake for a further hour.

7 To make the syrup, place ingredients in saucepan with 1½ cups water and bring to the boil. Reduce heat and let simmer for 10–15 minutes. Leave to cool before use. Pour cold syrup over baklava and cut into diamond shapes.

Serves 8 · Preparation 40 minutes · Cooking 1 hour 30 minutes

SHORTBREAD, SCONES & BUNS

Shortbread is much loved for its buttery flavour and distinctive crumbly texture. Shortbread originated in Scotland, as did scones. Scones are often eaten with jam (jelly) and cream as part of the famous Devonshire tea. Plain scones can be spiced up with ginger, currants, apple, dates or even cheese. Buns are another sweet bread treat that can be decorated for special occasions or enjoyed any time.

Hazelnut shortbreads

250g/9 oz butter, chopped
1½ cups plain (all-purpose) flour, sifted
45g/1½ oz hazelnuts, ground
¼ cup ground rice
¼ cup caster (berry) sugar
100g/3½ oz chocolate, melted

1   Preheat oven to 160°C/320°F.
2   Place butter, flour, hazelnuts and ground rice in a food processor and process until mixture resembles coarse breadcrumbs. Add sugar and process to combine.
3   Turn mixture onto a floured surface and knead lightly to make a pliable dough. Place dough between sheets of baking paper and roll out to 5mm/⅕ in thick. Using a 50mm/2 in fluted cutter, cut out rounds of dough and place 25mm/1 in apart on buttered baking trays (sheets). Bake for 20–25 minutes or until lightly browned. Stand on baking trays for 2–3 minutes before transferring to wire racks to cool.
4   Place melted chocolate in a plastic food bag, snip off one corner and pipe lines across each shortbread before serving.

Makes 40 · Preparation 20 minutes · Cooking 25 minutes

Hazelnut and coffee liqueur shortbreads

125g/4 oz butter
2 tablespoons icing (confectioner's) sugar
2 teaspoons coffee liqueur
2 tablespoons ground hazelnuts
¾ cup plain (all-purpose) flour, sifted

1   Preheat oven to 190°C/380°F.
2   Cream butter and sugar until soft. Add liqueur and hazelnuts and mix well. Fold in sifted flour.
3   Place the mixture into a piping bag fitted with fluted tube, pipe into fancy shapes onto a lightly buttered oven tray (sheet).
4   Bake for about 12 minutes or until pale golden brown.

Makes about 30 · Preparation 10 minutes · Cooking 12 minutes

ALMOND AND CHERRY SHORTBREADS

200g/7 oz butter
90g/3 oz caster (berry) sugar
¼ teaspoon vanilla extract
250g/9 oz plain (all-purpose) flour
60g/3 oz rice flour
¼ teaspoon baking powder
100g/3½ oz slivered almonds
100g/3½ oz glacé (glazed) cherries

1 Preheat oven to 190°C/380°F.

2 Cream butter, sugar and vanilla until light and fluffy.

3 Work in sifted dry ingredients, knead well on a lightly floured surface until mixture is smooth.

4 Press into a lightly buttered lamington tin (slice pan), mark into finger-length pieces, prick each bar with a fork and decorate with almonds and glacé (glazed) cherries.

5 Bake for about 30 minutes or until the shortbread is a light golden colour. Re-cut into fingers before serving. Store in an airtight container.

Makes 15–20 · Preparation 15 minutes · Cooking 20 minutes

SIMPLE SHORTBREAD COOKIES

1 cup butter
1 cup sugar
2 cups plain (all-purpose) flour

1 Preheat oven to 180°C/360°F.
2 Cream sugar and butter thoroughly. Add the flour and mix well. Turn out onto a lightly floured surface. Knead dough until it cracks on surface.
3 Roll out 6mm/¼ in thick and cut out with cookie cutter. Prick cookies with fork and place on unbuttered cookie trays (sheets).
4 Bake for about 40–50 minutes, or until lightly browned.

Makes about 24 · Preparation 10 minutes · Cooking 50 minutes

CHOCOLATE SHORTBREAD

300g/10½ oz unsalted butter
1 cup caster (berry) sugar
2½ cups plain (all-purpose) flour
5 tablespoons cocoa powder
¼ teaspoon bicarbonate of soda (baking soda)

1   Preheat oven to 180°C/360°F.

2   Butter and line base and sides of a 20cm x 30cm/8 x 12 in lamington (slice) pan. Beat butter and sugar in a bowl until pale.

3   Sift in flour, cocoa and bicarbonate of soda (baking soda) and beat slowly until just combined. Spread in pan and smooth with a spatula. Prick all over with a fork. Chill for 15 minutes.

4   Bake shortbread for 25 minutes or until firm to touch. While it's still hot, use a knife to score it into 12 rectangles.

5   Cool slightly, then remove from pan and cut into 12 pieces. Dust with extra cocoa before serving. Shortbread will keep for 3–4 days in an airtight container.

Makes 12 · Preparation 15 minutes · Cooking 25 minutes

SHORTBREAD TARTS WITH CREAM CHEESE

180g/6½ oz butter
½ cup icing (confectioner's) sugar
1 teaspoon vanilla extract
1½ cups plain (all-purpose) flour
2 tablespoons cornflour
(cornstarch)
⅛ teaspoon salt

Cream cheese filling
250g/9 oz cream cheese, softened
200g/7 oz sweetened condensed milk
⅓ cup freshly squeezed lemon juice
zest of 1 lemon
1 teaspoon vanilla extract
250g/9 oz fresh berries or fruit of choice

1   Preheat oven to 180°C/360°F.

2   Prepare a 36-cup mini muffin tin by buttering lightly.

3   Cream the butter and sugar well. Then add the vanilla, sifted flours and salt and mix until incorporated. Do not overmix. Divide the dough into 36 even pieces and place one ball of dough in the centre of each muffin tin. Press the dough up the sides of the individual muffin tin with your fingers so there is an indentation in the centre.

4   Once filled, place the tin, with the unbaked shells, in the freezer for about 10 minutes so the shortbread can become firm. (This will help to prevent the shortbread from puffing up during baking.)

5   Bake for approximately 18–20 minutes or until lightly browned. About halfway through the baking time, lightly prick the bottom of each shortbread with a fork. Check again after another 5 minutes and prick again if needed. Once they are fully baked, remove from oven and place on a wire rack to cool. When completely cooled, remove the tarts from the tin.

6   To make the cream cheese filling, beat the cream cheese until fluffy. Add the condensed milk, lemon juice, zest and vanilla, and process until smooth. Do not over-process or the filling will be too runny. Transfer the filling to a bowl, cover and refrigerate until serving time.

7   When ready to serve, fill the tart shells with the cream cheese filling and top with fresh berries or fruit of choice.

Makes about 36 • Preparation 35 minutes • Cooking 20 minutes

TRADITIONAL SCONES

2 cups self-raising flour
2 teaspoons sugar
30g/1 oz butter, cubed
¾ cup milk
1 tablespoon lemon juice

1   Combine flour and sugar in a bowl. Add butter and lightly rub into flour using fingertips.
2   Combine milk and lemon juice in a jug.
3   Make a well in the centre of the flour. Pour in milk and, using a knife, mix to a soft, sticky dough.
4   Turn onto a floured board and knead lightly. Shape into a rectangle and cut out scones with a cutter about 25mm/1 in high.
5   Cut a piece of baking paper to fit into a heavy-based frying pan (skillet) with a lid. Heat frying pan over low heat, place scones in pan, cover and cook for about 7–8 minutes each side or until golden.
6   Serve scones with butter and jam (jelly).

Makes 6–8 · Preparation 10 minutes · Cooking 16 minutes

Bran scones

1 cup wholemeal (whole wheat) self-raising flour
1 cup white self-raising flour
1 cup unprocessed bran
60g/2 oz butter
1 cup milk

1   Preheat oven to 180°C/360°F. Sift flours into a bowl, return husks from sifter to bowl, mix in bran. Rub in butter.
2   Make a well in the centre of dry ingredients, stir in enough milk to give a soft, sticky dough.
3   Turn dough onto lightly floured surface and knead lightly until smooth. Press dough out to 12mm/½ in thickness, cut into rounds with 5cm/2 in cutter.
4   Place scones into buttered slab tin, bake for 15 minutes or until golden brown.

Makes about 15 · Preparation 15 minutes · Cooking 15 minutes

HOT CROSS BUNS

3 sachets (7g/¼ oz) yeast
1 cup lukewarm milk
pinch of salt
2 tablespoons light brown sugar
1 teaspoon ground cinnamon
½ teaspoon ground nutmeg
¼ teaspoon ground allspice
2 eggs
4 cups plain (all-purpose) flour
2 tablespoons vegetable oil
2 tablespoons mixed peel
2 tablespoons sultanas (golden raisins)

Cross
½ cup plain (all-purpose) flour

Glaze
½ teaspoon gelatine
2 tablespoons icing (confectioner's) sugar
2 tablespoons warm low-fat milk

1   Place yeast in a large bowl. Pour in milk. Stand in warm place for 10 minutes or until frothy. Stir in salt, sugar and spices. Beat in eggs, one at a time. Stir in half the flour to make a soft dough. Beat in oil. Continue beating for 1 minute. Knead in remaining flour. Place dough in a lightly oiled bowl. Turn to coat with oil. Cover with plastic wrap. Stand in a warm place for 1 hour or until doubled in size.

2   Knead dough, working in mixed peel and sultanas (golden raisins) on a lightly floured surface. Roll into a log. Cut into 18 even-sized pieces. Shape pieces into buns. Place buns, 25mm/1 in apart, on buttered baking trays (sheets). Cover. Stand in a warm place for 20 minutes.

3   For the cross, place flour and ⅓ cup water in a bowl. Beat until smooth. Spoon cross mixture into a piping bag fitted with a small plain nozzle. Mark a cross on top each bun.

4   Preheat oven to 200°C/400°F. Bake buns for 15 minutes or until golden.

5   For the glaze, place all ingredients in a bowl. Mix until smooth. Brush warm buns with glaze.

Makes 18 · Preparation 1 hour 30 minutes · Cooking 15 minutes

DATE SCONES

500g/1 lb self-raising flour
1 teaspoon salt
2 teaspoons ground cinnamon
60g/2 oz butter
125g/4 oz chopped dates
30g/1 oz sugar
2 cups milk
1 egg, beaten
¼ cup milk

1 Preheat oven to 230°C/450°F.

2 Sift flour, salt and cinnamon then, using fingertips, rub butter into the flour mixture. Add dates and sugar. Make a well in the centre and add the 2 cups of milk all at once, stirring quickly and lightly to a soft dough.

3 Turn onto a lightly floured board and knead just enough to make a smooth surface. Pat into 12–18mm/½–¾ in thickness and, using a small scone (biscuit) cutter, cut into rounds.

4 Place on a floured baking tray (sheet). Brush tops with combined beaten egg and ¼ cup of milk and then bake for about 10 minutes.

Makes 12–16 • Preparation 20 minutes • Cooking 10 minutes

CHEESE SCONES

500g/1 lb self-raising flour
¼ teaspoon cayenne (red) pepper
1 teaspoon salt
60g/2 oz butter
1 tablespoon finely chopped onion
60g/2 oz cheddar cheese, grated
1 egg
¼ cup parsley, finely chopped
2 cups milk
1 egg, beaten
¼ cup milk

1   Preheat oven to 230°C/450°F.
2   Sift flour, pepper and salt then, using fingertips, rub butter into the flour mixture.
    Add onion, cheese, egg and parsley. Make a well in the centre and add the 2 cups
    of milk all at once, stirring quickly and lightly to a soft dough.
3   Turn onto a lightly floured board and knead just enough to make a smooth surface.
    Pat into 12–18mm/½–¾ in thickness and, using a small scone (biscuit) cutter, cut
    into rounds.
4   Place on a floured baking tray (sheet). Brush tops with combined beaten egg and
    ¼ cup of milk and then bake for about 10 minutes.

Makes 12–16 • Preparation 20 minutes • Cooking 10 minutes

Butterscotch buns

60g/2 oz butter, softened, plus 45g/1½ oz chilled butter
¾ cup brown sugar, packed
2 cups plain (all-purpose) flour
2 tablespoons granulated sugar
4 teaspoons baking powder
1 teaspoon salt
¾ cup milk
⅓ cup chopped nuts

1   Preheat oven to 220°C/430°F. Cream softened butter and brown sugar together in a small bowl. Set aside.

2   In a large bowl, combine flour, sugar, baking powder and salt. Cut in chilled butter until crumbly. Make a well in the centre.

3   Pour milk into the well. Stir to make a soft dough. Knead 8–10 times. Pat or roll out on lightly floured surface to 23–25cm/9–10 in square. Spread with brown sugar mixture.

4   Sprinkle with nuts. Roll up as you would a jam (jelly) roll. Pinch edge to seal. Cut into 12 slices. Place on buttered 20 x 20cm/8 x 8 in pan. Bake 15–20 minutes. While still hot, place a tray or plate over the pan and flip.

Makes 12 • Preparation 25 minutes • Cooking 20 minutes

APPLE SCONES

2 cups plain (all-purpose) flour
¼ cup granulated sugar
2 teaspoons baking powder
½ teaspoon bicarbonate of soda (baking soda)
½ teaspoon salt
45g/1½ oz butter, chilled
1 large apple, peeled and grated
½ cup milk

1   Preheat oven to 220°C/430°F. Combine flour, sugar, baking powder, bicarbonate of soda (baking soda) and salt in a large bowl. Cut in butter until crumbly.

2   Add apple and milk. Stir to form soft dough. Turn out on lightly floured surface. Knead gently 8–10 times. Pat into two 15cm/6 in circles. Place on buttered baking tray (sheet). Brush tops with milk. Sprinkle with sugar, then with cinnamon. Score each top into six pie-shaped wedges. Bake for 15 minutes until browned and risen. Serve warm with butter.

Makes 12 • Preparation 20 minutes • Cooking 15 minutes

CURRANT SCONES

2 cups plain (all-purpose) flour
¼ cup granulated sugar
4 teaspoons baking powder
½ teaspoon salt
45g/1½ oz butter, chilled
½ cup currants
1 egg
½ cup milk

1   Preheat oven to 220°C/430°F. In a large bowl, combine flour, sugar, baking
    powder and salt. Cut in butter until crumbly. Stir in currants. Make a well in
    the centre.

2   In a small bowl, beat egg until frothy. Stir in milk. Pour into the well. Stir with a
    fork to form soft dough. Turn out on lightly floured surface. Knead 8–10 times.
    Pat into 12–18mm/½–¾ in thickness and, using a small scone (biscuit) cutter, cut
    into rounds. Transfer to a buttered baking tray (sheet).

3   Brush tops with milk and sprinkle with sugar. Bake for 15 minutes until risen and
    browned slightly. Serve hot with butter and jam (jelly).

Makes 12 • Preparation 20 minutes • Cooking 15 minutes

GINGER SCONES

2 cups plain (all-purpose) flour
1 tablespoon granulated sugar
2 teaspoons baking powder
½ teaspoon bicarbonate of soda (baking soda)
¾ teaspoon salt
½ teaspoon ground cinnamon
½ teaspoon ground ginger
45g/1½ oz butter, chilled
1 egg
¼ cup (treacle) molasses
¼ cup buttermilk or sour milk

1 Preheat oven to 220°C/430°F. Measure flour, sugar, baking powder, bicarbonate of soda (baking soda), salt, cinnamon and ginger into a large bowl. Stir. Cut in butter until crumbly. Make a well in the centre.

2 In a small bowl, beat egg until frothy. Mix in treacle (molasses) and buttermilk. Pour into the well. Stir with fork to make a soft dough. Turn out on lightly floured surface. Knead lightly 8–10 times. Divide in half. Pat each half into a 15cm/6 in circle. Place on a buttered baking tray (sheet).

3 Brush tops with milk. Sprinkle with sugar. Score each top into six pie-shaped wedges. Bake for 30 minutes until risen and browned. Serve hot with lots of butter.

Makes 12 • Preparation 20 minutes • Cooking 30 minutes

MUFFINS & CUPCAKES

Muffins come in all flavours – from sweet to savoury. They are a great breakfast on the run and the perfect afternoon snack. Popular flavour additions are raspberries, dates, carrots and nuts. Cupcakes are an even sweeter treat, with the distinctive features of icing (frosting) and decorations. These mini cakes are the mainstay of children's parties, but also loved by the young at heart.

CARROT AND YOGHURT MUFFINS

375g/13 oz self-raising flour
½ teaspoon bicarbonate of soda (baking soda)
1 teaspoon ground mixed spice
90g/3 oz brown sugar
1 large carrot, grated
170g/6 oz sultanas (golden raisins)
200g/7 oz natural yoghurt
1 cup milk
45g/1½ oz butter, melted
2 eggs, lightly beaten

1   Preheat oven to 200°C/400°F. Sift flour, bicarbonate of soda (baking soda) and mixed spice into a large bowl. Add sugar, carrot and sultanas (golden raisins) and mix to combine.

2   Place yoghurt, milk, butter and eggs in a bowl and whisk to combine. Stir yoghurt mixture into flour mixture and mix until just combined. Spoon batter into lightly buttered muffin tins and bake for 20 minutes or until golden and cooked.

Makes 24 · Preparation 15 minutes · Cooking 20 minutes

OAT BRAN MUFFINS

1¼ cups oat bran
1 cup self-raising flour
½ cup milk
2 eggs, lightly beaten
¼ cup honey
3 tablespoons safflower oil

1   Preheat oven to 180°C/360°F. Mix oat bran and flour in large bowl.
2   Blend or process milk, eggs, honey and oil until smooth, add to flour mixture. Stir until just mixed.
3   Line a muffin tin with paper cups and fill with mixture.
4   Bake for 15 minutes or until a skewer inserted in centre comes out clean.

Makes 10 · Preparation 15 minutes · Cooking 15 minutes

Raspberry muffins

1 cup wholemeal (whole wheat) self-raising flour
1 cup white self-raising flour
½ cup bran
½ teaspoon bicarbonate of soda (baking soda)
1 teaspoon ground ginger
¾ cup buttermilk
⅓ cup orange juice concentrate
2 eggs
⅔ cup fresh, or frozen, partly thawed, raspberries

1   Preheat oven to 180°C/360°F. Sift dry ingredients into a bowl. Return any bran to
    the bowl.
2   Beat together buttermilk, orange juice and eggs. Pour into dry ingredients, all
    at once. Add raspberries and mix until just combined – take care not to overmix.
    Spoon into buttered muffin pans.
3   Bake for 20–25 minutes or until cooked when tested with a skewer.

Makes 10 · Preparation 15 minutes · Cooking 25 minutes

CHEESE AND BACON MUFFINS

2 cups plain (all-purpose) flour
1 tablespoon baking powder
¼ teaspoon salt
45g/1½ oz aged cheddar cheese, grated
4–5 bacon slices, cooked and crumbled
1 egg
1 cup milk
¼ cup olive oil

1   Preheat oven to 200°C/400°F. Put flour, baking powder, salt, cheese and bacon into a large bowl. Stir thoroughly. Make a well in the centre.

2   In a small bowl, beat egg lightly. Mix in milk and oil. Pour into the well. Stir only to moisten. Batter will be lumpy. Fill buttered muffin cups three-quarters full. Bake for 20–25 minutes. Let stand for 5 minutes. Remove from pan. Serve warm.

Makes 12 · Preparation 20 minutes · Cooking 25 minutes

DATE MUFFINS

1½ cups chopped dates
1 teaspoon bicarbonate of soda (baking soda)
1¾ cups plain (all-purpose) flour
1 teaspoon baking powder
½ teaspoon salt
½ cup chopped walnuts
2 eggs
¾ cup brown sugar, packed
¼ cup oil
1 teaspoon vanilla extract

1 Preheat oven to 200°C/400°F. Combine dates, ¾ cup boiling water and the bicarbonate of soda (baking soda) in a bowl. Set aside.

2 Combine flour, baking powder, salt and nuts in a second bowl. Stir well. Set aside.

3 In a mixing bowl, beat eggs until frothy. Slowly blend in sugar, oil and vanilla. Stir in date mixture. Pour in dry ingredients from second bowl. Stir just to combine. Don't worry if the batter is lumpy. Fill buttered muffin cups three-quarters full. Bake for 20–25 minutes. Remove from pan after 5 minutes.

Makes 16 • Preparation 20 minutes • Cooking 25 minutes

Pumpkin muffins

1½ cups plain (all-purpose) flour
1 teaspoon baking powder
1 teaspoon bicarbonate of soda (baking soda)
½ teaspoon salt
½ teaspoon ground cinnamon
½ teaspoon ground nutmeg
½ teaspoon ground ginger
½ cup raisins (dark raisins)
1 egg
¼ cup granulated sugar
⅓ cup olive oil
1 cup cooked pumpkin
½ cup milk
icing (confectioner's) sugar

1   Preheat oven to 200°C/400°F. Combine flour, baking powder, bicarbonate of soda (baking soda), salt, cinnamon, nutmeg, ginger and raisins (dark raisins) in a large bowl. Stir thoroughly. Make a well in the centre.

2   In a small bowl, beat egg until frothy. Mix in sugar, oil, pumpkin and milk. Pour into well. Stir only to moisten. Batter will be lumpy. Fill buttered muffin cups three-quarters full. Bake for 15–20 minutes. Let stand 5 minutes. Remove from pan. Serve warm. Dust with icing (confectioner's) sugar.

Makes 12 • Preparation 25 minutes • Cooking 20 minutes

BERRY CRUMBLE MUFFINS

1 cup self-raising flour, sifted
1 cup plain (all-purpose) flour, sifted
1 teaspoon baking powder
½ cup brown sugar
¾ cup milk
¼ cup canola oil
2 eggs, lightly beaten
1 cup frozen mixed berries

Crumble topping
2 tablespoons plain (all-purpose) flour
30g/1 oz butter, cut into cubes
2 tablespoons brown sugar

1   Preheat oven to 180°C/360°F. Butter 12 medium muffin tins.

2   In a medium bowl sift together the flours and baking powder and stir in the sugar.

3   In a separate bowl, mix the milk, oil and eggs together. Make a well in the centre of the dry ingredients and pour in the milk mixture.

4   Add the berries and mix until just combined.

5   To make the crumble topping, place the flour and butter in a medium bowl and rub in the butter with your fingertips until the mixture resembles breadcrumbs. Stir in the sugar and set aside.

6   Spoon the dough into muffin tins and sprinkle with the crumble mixture. Bake for 20–25 minutes or until muffins are cooked when tested with skewer. Turn onto wire racks to cool.

Makes 12 · Preparation 20 minutes · Cooking 25 minutes

CARROT MUFFINS

1½ cups plain (all-purpose) flour, sifted
2 teaspoons baking powder
½ teaspoon salt
3 tablespoons sugar
1 teaspoon ground cinnamon
1 teaspoon ground nutmeg
1 cup grated carrot
¼ cup currants
1 egg
½ cup milk
75g/2½ oz butter, melted

1   Preheat oven to 180°C/360°F. Butter 12 medium muffin tins.
2   In a medium bowl, sift together flour, baking powder, salt, sugar and spices. Mix in grated carrot and currants.
3   Place egg, milk and butter in a small bowl and whisk to combine. Pour milk mixture into dry ingredients and mix with a fork until ingredients are just combined, do not over-mix.
4   Spoon mixture into 12 buttered muffin tins. Bake for 20–25 minutes or until muffins are cooked when tested with a skewer. Turn onto wire racks to cool.

Makes 12 · Preparation 20 minutes · Cooking 25 minutes

CHOCOLATE FRUITY CUPCAKES

125g/4 oz butter
½ cup sugar
2 eggs
1 cup sultanas (golden raisins)
90g/3 oz glacé (glazed) cherries, chopped
¼ cup chocolate chips, chopped
1½ cups self-raising flour
¼ cup cocoa powder
½ cup milk

Chocolate icing (frosting)
1½ cups icing (confectioner's) sugar
1 tablespoon cocoa powder
1 teaspoon melted butter
2 tablespoons milk

1   Preheat oven to 180°C/360°F.

2   Cream butter and sugar until light and fluffy, add eggs, one at a time, beating well after each addition.

3   Fold in sultanas (golden raisins), chopped cherries and chocolate then flour, cocoa and milk alternately.

4   Drop teaspoons of mixture into well-buttered deep cupcake pans or paper cases. Bake for about 15 minutes

5   Sift icing (confectioner's) sugar and cocoa into a small basin, add melted butter and milk and beat until smooth.

6   Spread chocolate icing (frosting) over top of cakes while hot, then top with extra sultanas, cherries and chocolate to garnish.

Makes about 30 • Preparation 20 minutes • Cooking 15 minutes

CUTE BUG CUPCAKES

270g/9½ oz butter, softened
1 cup caster (berry) sugar
3 eggs
½ cup buttermilk
1½ cups self-raising flour, sifted
1 teaspoon vanilla extract

Topping
1½ cups icing (confectioner's) sugar
90g/3 oz butter, softened
6 drops vanilla extract
red food colouring
18 mini white marshmallows
liquorice strap

1   Preheat the oven to 160°C/320°F. Line a 12-cup muffin tin with cupcake papers.

2   Using an electric mixer, cream the butter and sugar, until light and fluffy. Add the eggs one at a time, beating well after each addition.

3   Add buttermilk, flour and vanilla extract and stir to combine. Beat with an electric mixer until light and creamy.

4   Divide the mixture evenly between the cupcake papers. Bake for about 20 minutes, until risen and firm to the touch. Allow to cool for a few minutes, then transfer to a wire rack. Allow to cool fully before icing (frosting).

5   To make the topping, combine icing (confectioner's) sugar, butter and vanilla extract and stir with a spoon until mixed together and mixture is light and fluffy. Tint the icing to the required shade of red with the food colouring, then spread evenly onto the cupcakes, making a nice hump for each ladybird's back.

6   Cut the liquorice into thin strips and make lines down the centre of each cake for the wings. Cut a cross section of marshmallow with scissors and cut a half circle of liquorice for the head and spots for the back. Place this on the half circle of liquorice to make the face. Place liquorice spots on the back to make the ladybird spots and small pieces of liquorice on the marshmallows for the eyes.

Makes about 18 • Preparation 40 minutes • Cooking 20 minutes

VANILLA SPRINKLES CUPCAKES

3 eggs
1 cup butter, softened
1 cup caster (berry) sugar
½ cup milk
1½ cups self-raising flour, sifted
1 teaspoon vanilla extract
1 teaspoon cocoa powder

Topping
½ cup icing (confectioner's) sugar
sprinkles (or 100s & 1000s)

1   Preheat the oven to 160°C/320°F. Line a 12-cupcake pan with cupcake papers.
     In a medium-sized bowl, lightly beat the eggs, add butter and sugar, then mix until
     light and fluffy.

2   Add milk and flour and stir to combine. Beat with an electric mixer for
     2 minutes, until light and creamy.

3   Divide the mixture in half, and add the vanilla to one half and cocoa powder to the
     other, then divide evenly between the cake papers. Bake for 18–20 minutes until
     risen and firm to touch. Allow to cool for a few minutes and then transfer to a
     wire rack. Allow to cool fully before icing (frosting).

4   To make the topping, combine icing (confectioner's) sugar and ¾ tablespoon hot
     water in a small bowl, and mix with a wooden spoon. Spoon onto cupcakes.
     Tip sprinkles onto a small plate and gently press each cupcake into the sprinkles.

Makes 12 · Preparation 12 minutes · Cooking 20 minutes

CHERRY-TOP CUPCAKES

3 eggs
1 cup butter, softened
1 cup caster (berry) sugar
½ cup milk
1½ cups self-raising flour, sifted
1 teaspoon vanilla extract
1 tablespoon cocoa powder

Topping
1 cup dark (semi-sweet) chocolate drops
15g/½ oz butter, at room temperature
⅓ cup thickened (whipping) cream
6 glacé (glazed) cherries, halved

1   Preheat the oven to 160°C/320°F. Line a 12-cupcake pan with cupcake papers. In a medium-sized bowl, lightly beat the eggs, add butter and sugar, then mix until light and fluffy.

2   Add milk, flour, vanilla and cocoa powder, and stir to combine. Beat with an electric mixer for 2 minutes, until light and creamy.

3   Divide the mixture evenly between the cupcake papers. Bake for 18–20 minutes until risen and firm to touch. Allow to cool for a few minutes and then transfer to a wire rack. Allow to cool fully before icing (frosting).

4   To make the topping, combine the chocolate and butter in a medium-sized saucepan over a medium heat. As the mixture begins to melt, reduce heat to low, stirring constantly, until melted. Remove from heat, add cream, and stir. Rest for 10 minutes – the mixture will be firm and velvety in consistency.

5   Spoon into a piping bag with a broad nozzle, and pipe onto cupcakes in a spiral. Top with cherry pieces.

Makes 12 • Preparation 12 minutes • Cooking 20 minutes

TOFFEE MERINGUE CUPCAKES

3 eggs
180g/6½ oz butter, softened
1 cup caster (berry) sugar
½ cup milk
2 cups self-raising flour, sifted
1 teaspoon vanilla extract
½ cup peanuts, crushed

Butter cream topping
1 cup icing (confectioner's) sugar
180g/6½ oz butter, at room temperature

Meringue topping
3 egg whites
¼ teaspoon cream of tartar
½ cup sugar

Toffee
½ cup caster (berry) sugar

1   Preheat the oven to 160°C/320°F. Line a 12-cupcake pan with cupcake papers. In a medium-sized bowl, lightly beat the eggs, add butter and sugar, then mix until light and fluffy.

2   Add milk, flour and vanilla, and stir to combine. Beat with an electric mixer for 2 minutes, until light and creamy. Fold in crushed peanuts.

3   Divide the mixture evenly between the cake papers. Bake for 18–20 minutes until risen and firm to touch. Allow to cool for a few minutes and then transfer to a wire rack. Allow to cool fully before icing (frosting).

4   To make the butter cream topping, combine half the icing (confectioner's) sugar and butter, mix with a wooden spoon, add remaining sugar and butter and beat with the spoon until light and fluffy. Spread onto cupcakes.

5   To make the meringue topping, create a double boiler by bringing 2 cups of water to the boil in a medium-sized saucepan, and reduce heat slightly. Place a glass bowl into the saucepan that is large enough to fit into the pan while still resting on the top rim.

6   Add egg whites to hot bowl and whisk until foaming. Add cream of tartar and whisk until fluffy. Pour in sugar slowly in one stream, whisking constantly to form stiff peaks.

7   Spread mixture onto a baking tray (sheet) and lightly brown under the grill (broiler) for 1–2 minutes. Place in the oven for 3 minutes, then open the oven door slightly and leave meringue for a further 3 minutes.

8   To make the toffee, place ½ cup caster (berry) sugar evenly on a greaseproof-paper-lined baking tray, and bake at 200°C/400°F for approximately 25 minutes until toffee consistency forms. Cool until hardened.

9   Crumble the meringue topping onto the cupcakes, then crumble the toffee on top.

Makes 12 · Preparation 12 minutes · Cooking 30 minutes

STICKY DATE CUPCAKES

2 eggs
130g/4½ oz butter, at room temperature
¾ cup caster (berry) sugar
1 cup self-raising flour, sifted
400g/14 oz dates, chopped
2 teaspoons instant coffee powder
1 teaspoon bicarbonate of soda (baking soda)
1 teaspoon vanilla extract
1 cup ground almond flour
½ cup walnuts, finely chopped

Topping
1 cup packed light-brown sugar
60g/2 oz unsalted butter
1 teaspoon vanilla extract
45g/1½ oz dates

1   Preheat the oven to 160°C/320°F. Line a 12-cupcake pan with cupcake papers. In a medium-sized bowl, lightly beat the eggs, add butter and sugar, then mix until light and fluffy.

2   Add ¾ cup water and the flour, and stir to combine. Add remaining cupcake ingredients. Mix with a wooden spoon for 2 minutes, until light and creamy.

3   Divide the mixture evenly between the cake papers. Bake for 18–20 minutes until risen and firm to touch. Allow to cool for a few minutes and then transfer to a wire rack. Allow to cool fully before icing (frosting).

4   To make the topping, combine sugar, butter, vanilla and 2 tablespoon water in a saucepan. Bring to a simmer over medium-low heat, stirring constantly. Without stirring again, simmer for 1 minute. Remove from heat, allow to cool and spoon onto cakes. Top each cupcake with a date and more topping. Heat the top of each cupcake with a blowtorch, being careful not to scorch the paper or the dates.

Makes 12 • Preparation 12 minutes • Cooking 20 minutes

CARAMEL NOUGAT CUPCAKES

3 eggs
180g/6½ oz butter, softened
1 cup caster (berry) sugar
½ cup milk
1½ cups self-raising flour
1 teaspoon vanilla extract

Topping
1 cup icing (confectioner's) sugar
180g/6½ oz butter, at room temperature
100g/3½ oz nougat, chopped

1   Preheat the oven to 160°C/320°F. Line a 12-cupcake pan with cupcake papers. In a medium-sized bowl, lightly beat the eggs, add butter and sugar, then mix until light and fluffy.

2   Add milk, flour and vanilla, and stir to combine. Beat with an electric mixer for 2 minutes, until light and creamy.

3   Divide the mixture evenly between the cake papers. Bake for 18–20 minutes until risen and firm to touch. Allow to cool for a few minutes and then transfer to a wire rack. Allow to cool fully before icing (frosting).

4   To make the topping, combine icing (confectioner's) sugar and butter in a small bowl, mix and add chopped nougat. Stir and spoon onto cupcakes in mounds.

Makes 12 · Preparation 12 minutes · Cooking 20 minutes

PISTACHIO ZINGER CUPCAKE

3 eggs
180g/6½ oz butter, softened
1 cup caster (berry) sugar
½ cup yoghurt
2 cups self-raising flour, sifted
1 teaspoon vanilla extract
1 zucchini (courgette), grated
juice of ½ a lime
zest of 1 lime
½ cup pistachios

Topping
1 cup icing (confectioner's) sugar
180g/6½ oz butter, at room temperature
zest of 1 lime
½ cup pistachios

1   Preheat the oven to 160°C/320°F. Line a 12-cupcake pan with cupcake papers. In a medium-sized bowl, lightly beat the eggs, add butter and sugar, then mix until light and fluffy.

2   Add yoghurt, flour and vanilla, and stir to combine. Beat with an electric mixer for 2 minutes, until light and creamy. Add zucchini (courgette), lime juice, zest and pistachios and mix through.

3   Divide the mixture evenly between the cake papers. Bake for 18–20 minutes until risen and firm to touch. Allow to cool for a few minutes and then transfer to a wire rack. Allow to cool fully before icing (frosting).

4   To make the topping, combine half the icing (confectioner's) sugar and butter, mix with a wooden spoon, then add remaining icing sugar and butter, and beat with the spoon until light and fluffy. Add lime zest and half of the pistachios and mix through.

5   Apply icing to cupcakes with the back of a spoon or a small spatula, and sprinkle each cake with a few of the remaining nuts.

Makes 12 • Preparation 12 minutes • Cooking 20 minutes

WEIGHTS AND MEASURES

Although recipes have been tested using the Australian Standard 250ml cup, 20ml tablespoon and 5ml teaspoon, they will work just as well with the US and Canadian 8fl oz cup, or the UK 300ml cup. We have used graduated cup measures in preference to tablespoon measures so that proportions are always the same. Where tablespoon measures have been given, they are not crucial measures, so using the smaller tablespoon of the US or UK will not affect the recipe's success. But we all agree on the teaspoon size.

For breads, cakes and pastries, the only area which might cause concern is where eggs are used, as proportions will then vary. If working with a 250ml or 300ml cup, use large eggs (65g/2¼ oz), adding a little more liquid to the recipe for 300ml cup measures if it seems necessary. Use medium-sized eggs (60g/2 oz) with an 8fl oz cup measure. A graduated set of measuring cups and spoons is recommended, the cups in particular for measuring dry ingredients. Remember to level such ingredients to ensure an accurate quantity.

Oven Temperatures

The Celsius temperatures given here are not exact; they have been rounded off and are given as a guide only. Follow the manufacturer's temperature guide, relating it to oven description given in the recipe. Remember gas ovens are hottest at the top, electric ovens at the bottom and convection-fan forced ovens are usually even throughout. We've included Regulo numbers for gas cookers, which may assist. To convert °C to °F multiply °C by 9 and divide by 5 then add 32.

	C°	F°	Gas Regulo
Very slow	120	250	1
Slow	150	300	2
Moderately slow	160	320	3
Moderate	180	360	4
Moderately hot	190–200	380–400	5–6
Hot	210–220	410–430	6–7
Very hot	230	450	8
Super hot	250–290	475–550	9–10

English Measures

English measurements are similar to Australian with two exceptions: the English cup measures 300ml/10½fl oz, whereas the American and Australian cup measure 250ml/8¾fl oz. The English tablespoon (the Australian dessertspoon) measures 14.8ml/½ fl oz against the Australian tablespoon of 20ml/¾fl oz.

American Measures

The American tablespoon is equal to 14.8ml/½fl oz, the teaspoon is 5ml/⅙fl oz. The cup measure is 250ml/8¾fl oz.

Dry Measures

All the measures are level, so when you have filled a cup or spoon, level it off with the edge of a knife. The scale below is the 'cook's equivalent'; it is not an exact conversion of metric to imperial measurement. To calculate the exact metric equivalent yourself, multiply ounces by 28.349523 to obtain grams, or divide grams by 28.349523 to obtain ounces.

Metric grams (g), kilograms (kg)	Imperial ounces (oz), pound (lb)	Metric grams (g), kilograms (kg)	Imperial ounces (oz), pound (lb)
15g	$\frac{1}{2}$ oz	240g	$8\frac{1}{2}$ oz
20g	$\frac{3}{4}$ oz	315g	11 oz
30g	1 oz	350g	12 oz
60g	2 oz	375g	13 oz
90g	3 oz	400g	14 oz
100g	$3\frac{1}{2}$ oz	425g	15 oz
125g	4 oz	450g	16 oz
150g	5 oz	1000g/1kg	2 lb
170g	6 oz	$1\frac{1}{2}$kg	$3\frac{1}{3}$ lb
200g	7 oz		

Liquid Measures

Metric millilitres (ml)	Imperial fluid ounce (fl oz)	Cup and Spoon
5ml	$\frac{1}{6}$ fl oz	1 teaspoon
20ml	$\frac{2}{3}$ fl oz	1 tablespoon
30ml	1 fl oz	1 tbsp + 2 tsp
55ml	2 fl oz	
63ml	$2\frac{1}{4}$ fl oz	$\frac{1}{4}$ cup
85ml	3 fl oz	
115ml	4 fl oz	
125ml	$4\frac{1}{2}$ fl oz	$\frac{1}{2}$ cup
150ml	$5\frac{1}{4}$ fl oz	
188ml	$6\frac{2}{3}$ fl oz	$\frac{3}{4}$ cup
225ml	$8\frac{3}{4}$ fl oz	
250ml	8 fl oz	1 cup
300ml	$10\frac{1}{2}$ fl oz	
370ml	13 fl oz	
400ml	14 fl oz	
438ml	$15\frac{1}{2}$ fl oz	$1\frac{3}{4}$ cups
455ml	16 fl oz	
500ml	$17\frac{1}{2}$ fl oz	2 cups
570ml	20 fl oz	
1 litre	$35\frac{1}{3}$ fl oz	4 cups

INDEX